FROM RECONQUEST TO EMPIRE

BORZOI BOOKS ON LATIN AMERICA

General Editor

LEWIS HANKE

UNIVERSITY OF MASSACHUSETTS, AMHERST

FROM RECONQUEST TO EMPIRE:
The Iberian Background to Latin American History

———◆———

EDITED WITH AN INTRODUCTION BY

H. B. JOHNSON, JR.
University of Virginia

ALFRED · A · KNOPF / New York

THIS IS A BORZOI BOOK
PUBLISHED BY ALFRED A KNOPF, INC.

Library of Congress Catalog Card Number: 79–114567
Manufactured in the United States

FIRST EDITION

9 8 7 6 5 4 3 2 1

Dedicated to

CHARLES JULIAN BISHKO

Acknowledgments

I am grateful to Dauril Alden, Ursula Lamb, and Richard Morse, all of whom were good enough to read the Introduction and favor me with their comments, as well as to my graduate students at Yale who bore with the text in its preliminary form and responded with a number of acute suggestions. My particular thanks are due to Julian Bishko who accompanied the book from beginning to end with cordial, constructive criticism, and to Lewis Hanke who was generous enough to entrust a challenging topic to a young colleague. Robert Williams of the Yale Map Laboratory kindly prepared the maps, Carl Herbold made a preliminary translation of certain parts of the Sánchez-Albornoz selection, and Dona Carolina Cortesão was gracious enough to review my translation of her late husband's essay. To all of them I am indebted; responsibility for the final result, however, is solely mine.

Charlottesville, Virginia   H. B. J., Jr.

Contents

FROM RECONQUEST TO EMPIRE

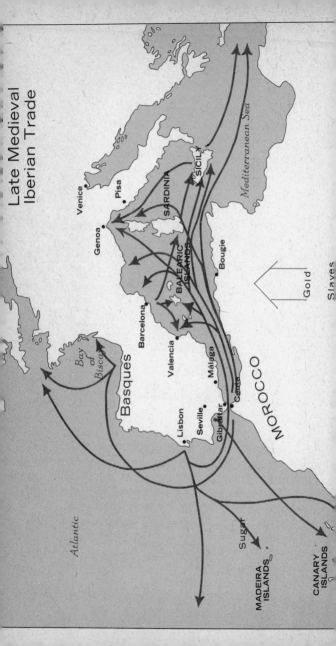

Late Medieval
Iberian Trade

INTRODUCTION

*These Iberian pioneers . . . expanded the horizon,
and thereby potentially the domain, of the society
they represented until it came to embrace all the
habitable lands and navigable seas of the globe. It is
owing in the first instance to this Iberian energy that
Western Christendom has grown, like a grain of
mustard seed in the parable, until it has become "the
Great Society": a tree in whose branches all the
nations of the Earth have come and lodged.*
— A. J. Toynbee, A Study of History

Merging Traditions

Compared to the empires previously known to world
history, those created by Spain and Portugal were unprecedented in the rapidity of their formation, in their immen-
sity, and in the unique effects that they had on the future
course of human development. During the centuries prior
to Columbus, the indigenous civilizations of America had
had tenuous and intermittent contact across the Pacific
with Asia, as had Asia via the steppes with Europe; but,
aside from the isolated landfalls made by the Vikings on
the coast of North America, the Atlantic had long remained a hiatus in this chain of world interrelationships. It
was the forging of this last link by the Iberian nations at

the end of the fifteenth century that gave birth to the one, problematic, inescapable world of today.

Charles Verlinden, the Belgian historian, has pointed out that the unprecedented size of these Iberian empires, as well as the impulse for profit and proselytization, which marked their creation, makes it impossible to characterize them as simple revivals of the imperialism of classical antiquity. Unlike the empires of the nineteenth and twentieth centuries, they were mercantile structures, called into being to furnish luxury goods to a growing market rather than as outlets to absorb the ever-expanding production of industrial capitalism. In character and structure, on the other hand, they bore a close resemblance to the Mediterranean empires that were created during the eleventh and twelfth centuries by the great trading cities of northern Italy—Genoa, Pisa, Venice—in the wake of the Crusades.[1] Yet, despite this resemblance, they cannot be regarded as mere continuations of the latter; other contrasting traditions also had a decisive part to play in their formation. In addition to the practices of mercantile capitalism that had been developed in the medieval Mediterranean, the Iberian empires inherited the habits of territorial conquest and lordship that had been forged by the Castilians and the Portuguese during the centuries of intermittent warfare against the Moors.

Both traditions were, in fact, twin aspects of the revival of Europe, which began soon after the collapse of the Carolingian Empire, and both of them were realized under the ideological aegis of crusade. Such apparent similarities, however, were not enough to ensure that their collaboration in the later trans-Atlantic expansion would be harmonious. They were, in fact, uneasy partners. The Mediterranean tradition, dominant initially, assumed a larger role in the Portuguese expansion and was preserved longer in the trading "factories" that were established along the

---

[1] Charles Verlinden, "Le Problème de la continuité en histoire coloniale," *Revista de Indias*, XI (1951), 219–236.

African coast and in India; while the Iberian tradition of conquest and lordship, recessive at first, emerged triumphant in the conquest of Mexico and Peru and gave to the Spanish Empire in America its permanent and indelible stamp.

What was the genesis of these traditions? How and why did they emerge? And what did the subsequent dialectic between them contribute to the birth of Latin America?

The Iberian Heritage

The men who conquered America were the cultural heirs of the *reconquistadores* of Iberia, warriors like the Cid who reestablished Christian culture and society behind a moving frontier, which they pushed from the mountains of northern Spain to the Straits of Gibraltar during some four centuries of intermittent struggle against the Moors. Driven principally by a hunger for land and booty, these *reconquistadores* left in their wake, not only a belief in personal valor as the surest road to wealth and honor, but a frontier ethic as well, which was kept alive in the late medieval ballad tradition and the romances of chivalry.

This process of reconquest took the form of a series of sluggish pulsations southward alternating with periods of quiescence and coexistence. Each outward pulsation was largely determined by population pressure and hunger for booty, while the contractions and relaxations were imposed by geographic barriers and Muslim military reaction. Following each outward thrust, a period of territorial digestion set in, during which the newly conquered area was settled and population accumulated until new pangs of land hunger led to a repetition of the cycle.

Historians generally distinguish three main stages in this expansion (see map): a first push lasting from about 850 to 950, which took Christian forces into the valley of the Duero river and was followed by a Muslim military reaction under the leadership of Almanzor; a second thrust

lasting from about 1050 to 1100 into the basin of the
Tagus, which was secured by the conquest of the strategic
city of Toledo in 1085; and finally, beginning in 1212, a
third drive into the valley of the Guadalquivir incorporating all of Andalusia except for the small Muslim kingdom
(*taifa*) of Granada, which was suffered to exist until the
reign of Ferdinand and Isabella.

The manner in which this last great territorial ingestion
was settled has been studied in detail by Júlio González,[2]
and what happened here in Extremadura and Andalusia is
relevant to an understanding of similar events which later
took place in the New World, for it was precisely from
these regions that most of the first conquistadors and
settlers came. Eminent rights over the conquered territory
fell to the Crown; but to hasten the process of settlement
the king granted out the land to various subordinate
authorities—to the military orders which had assisted him
in the conquest (Calatrava, Santiago, and Alcántara), to
the archbishopric of Toledo, as well as to a variety of
municipal councils (*cabildos*), which were established in
the newly conquered area. The territory allotted to the
cabildos was further subdivided into four parts: one reserved for the king and his household, one for the local
church, one for the lay and ecclesiastical magnates, while
the remaining lands were granted to the other settlers on
the basis of their status—*caballerías* for the knights and
smaller plots, or *peonías*, for the foot-soldiers. Preexisting
latifundia of Roman or Moorish origin were generally
preserved, since the ecology of the region discouraged the
creation of a multiplicity of small holdings and since
settlers were too scarce, in any case, to occupy all the land
available. Indeed the majority of northern immigrants went
into the cities and towns from which the Moorish population had already been expelled, thus perpetuating and
reinforcing the ancient Andalusian pattern of relatively

---

[2] Júlio González, *Repartimiento de Sevilla,* 2 vols. (Madrid,
1951), I, 234–324.

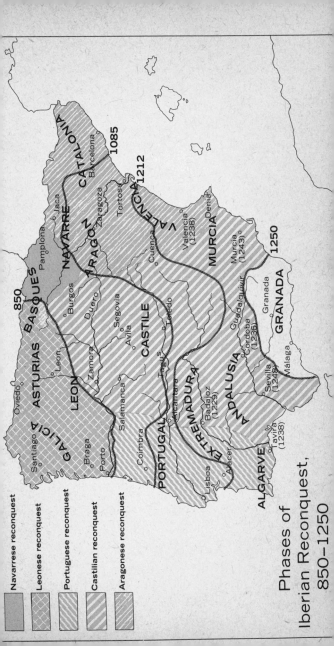

Phases of
Iberian Reconquest,
850–1250

Navarrese reconquest

Leonese reconquest

Portuguese reconquest

Castilian reconquest

Aragonese reconquest

large urban centers set amidst a sparsely populated countryside, best suited to ranching and sheep herding.

Spanish historians incline to view this long process of
southward expansion as having decisively influenced the
subsequent character of Spanish society. In Selection 1, for
example, Claudio Sánchez-Albornoz elaborates the view
that these centuries of reconquest were responsible for
forming the "world outlook" of the hidalgos, which they
later carried, as conquistadors, to the New World. He
argues that the enormous amounts of land and booty,
which each cycle of conquest placed at the disposal of the
Crown, made it almost impossible for the knights along the
frontier to resist the temptation of serving a king who was
sure to reward them handsomely with property and spoils
of office in the newly conquered territory:

> The lands along the frontier offered the common
> people an opportunity for enrichment and social bet-
> terment; and thus there triumphed an economy of
> looting, linked to military initiative, to daring, to royal
> favor, and to admission into royal service.[3]

This tendency for the most dynamic sectors of society to
gravitate "like satellites" about the monarch produced a
social and political organization that set medieval Castile
on a course of development radically different from that
followed by the rest of Christian Europe in at least two
important respects. First, the overwhelming importance
that the constant warfare gave to royal leadership made it
impossible for Castilian society to evolve a decentralized,
feudal basis, as did medieval England or France. Consequently, there never developed the traditions of local initiative and responsibility that were so important in bringing
about the development of constitutional government elsewhere in Europe. Second, the mobile, warlike style of life,
which the Reconquest fostered, gravely impeded the devel-

---

[3] Claudio Sánchez-Albornoz, *España, un enigma histórico*, 2
vols. (Buenos Aires, 1956), I, 684.

opment of a native bourgeoisie. The towns that were erected in the wake of the *reconquistadores* were military and religious centers, not places of trade; and the quick profits that could be had from raids across the frontier led the Christian population to despise industry, commerce, and manual labor. These were looked upon as inferior occupations, best suited to Moors and Jews who could not take part in military activities:

> The bravest, most adventuresome men, those with the greatest ambition and daring . . . always turned their energies to military service. Industry and commerce got only the residual effort which the urban populace did not devote to military activity.[4]

In contrast to this dynamic, socioeconomic interpretation, Américo Castro, working mainly from literary sources, suggests a more static, ideological interpretation of *hidalguismo* in Selection 9. In his view the existence of three mutually exclusive religions in medieval Spain (Christianity, Islam, and Judaism) produced not so much a society stratified into classes, as one separated into castes, each with its own peculiar ethos and occupations: the Jews as doctors, intellectuals, and money lenders; the Moors as artisans and small tenant farmers; while the Christian hidalgos monopolized the ownership of land and the administrative posts, both civil and ecclesiastical. Disdaining to engage in any of the occupations reserved to the lower castes, the hidalgo instead sought his identity in an obsessive preoccupation with questions of status and honor, which was later carried over into his treatment of the native populations of the New World.

Whatever may have been the effect of the Reconquest on shaping the collective psyche of the hidalgo, the closing of the frontier with the end of the Reconquest presented this group with a serious practical problem of readjustment. Cut off from the income of land and booty to which they

---

[4] *Ibid.*, p. 682.

had grown accustomed, they were forced to make fundamental changes in their way of life. Some of them sallied forth to make their way as knights-errant on the "chivalry circuit" of European courts. Others clung to their former habits of life by joining one of the factions, led by members of the nobility, that terrorized the towns and threatened the throne in a kind of endemic civil strife that kept late medieval Castile in a state of chronic unrest. The bulk of them, however, turned to ranching (described by Charles Julian Bishko in Selection 5) and especially to raising the sheep whose wool enjoyed a rapidly expanding market in late medieval Europe. Deprived of the pleasures of despoiling their Moorish neighbors, these leftover *reconquistadores* had to content themselves with fleecing their sheep.

Sheep herding had been practiced on the Iberian *meseta* (plateau) since ancient times, but the surging growth that it experienced in the century after the end of the Reconquest was made possible by two important developments in the late thirteenth century. The first of these was the administrative unification and pacification of Castile and Andalusia brought about by the final reconquest of the south. For the first time sheep owners could move their flocks with real safety along the great *cañadas* (sheep walks), which extended the length of Spain from the summer pastures in the northern mountains to the winter grazing grounds in the Guadalquivir valley. The second factor was the adoption, at the urging of Genoese merchants, of a variety of North African sheep known as merino, which produced an especially fine quality of wool much in demand in the centers of European cloth manufacture.[5]

The rapid growth of wool production, which these two developments brought about, had repercussions in nearly all aspects of Castilian life. Economically, there developed

---

[5] Robert S. Lopez, "The Origin of the Merino Sheep," *Joshua Starr Memorial Volume* (New York, 1953).

a typically colonial infrastructure dependent upon the sale in foreign markets of a single product that the government favored to the detriment of other industries because of the taxes which it collected on the exports. Socially, the wealth, which the wool industry brought to Andalusian nobles and military orders who owned most of the sheep, made late medieval Castile into one of the greatest luxury markets in Europe at that time. Politically, it allowed this same group to gain control of royal policy through the organization called the *Mesta,* which it created to defend its interests. Finally, the emphasis on sheep herding retarded the development of Spanish agriculture by monopolizing large tracts of land that could otherwise have been devoted to the raising of grain.[6] In fact, by the time of Ferdinand and Isabella, the large areas reserved for sheep walks had caused a noticeable scarcity of agricultural land in southwestern Spain, one of the main reasons for the extensive emigration from that area to the Indies after the discovery of America.[7] In sum, then, the spread of transhumance preserved and consolidated an economy, a society, and an ethos that had already been sketched out during the years of reconquest.

Such a society, undercommercialized and colonial in structure, inevitably invited exploitation by more developed centers of trade. Thus began the *mariage de convenance* that brought increasing numbers of Italian merchants and bankers into the peninsula during the late middle ages and that laid the foundations for an uneasy alliance between the Iberian heritage of conquest and the Mediterranean experience of mercantile capitalism. The fusion of these two traditions furnished the immediate background to the discovery, conquest, and settlement of the New World.

---

[6] Jaime Vicens Vives, *História económica de España* (Barcelona, 1959), pp. 231–232.

[7] Mário Góngora, "Regímen senorial y rural en al Extremadura de la órden de Santiago en el momento de la emigración a Indias," *Jahrbuch für Geschichte von Staat, Wirtschaft und Gesellschaft Lateinamerikas,* I (1964), 1–29.

The importance of this association in the destinies of Iberia can best be gauged from the change in direction taken by the Reconquest when it was resumed in the fifteenth century. Without the admixture of Italian commercial influences, the Portuguese conquest of Ceuta (1415) and the subsequent Castilian war against Granada (1482–1492) would most likely have led to little more than the conquest of the petty kingdoms which lined the North African coast, in a fashion similar to that in which the various *taifa* kingdoms of Andalusia had been incorporated during the reconquest of the peninsula. Instead of this, however, the push into Africa was deflected by the momentum of a westward movement coming from the Mediterranean and spearheaded by Genoese merchants. They and their associates bore the renewed impulse of conquest to the far shore of the Atlantic where Iberian knights found, not dusty North African villages, but unbounded horizons of exotic kingdoms richer in booty and slaves than anything they could ever have imagined in Andalusia or Morocco.

The Mediterranean Prototype

In the beginning this Mediterranean movement, like the Reconquest with which it merged, formed another aspect of the expansion of Europe, which began shortly after the collapse of the Carolingian Empire. Led by Italian seamen and Norman adventurers, this European push into areas under the control of Islam eventually culminated in the Crusades, medieval Christendom's first experiment in overseas empire. While the knights from northern Europe carved out estates and principalities for themselves in the Holy Land, the Italian cities, which had supplied the capital, outfitted their ships, and provisioned the armies, took payment in the form of commercial privileges and trading "factories" (*fondacos*), which they set up in the newly conquered areas. To supervise their trade with these outposts, they created various agencies, such as the Geno-ese *Officium Gazaire,* regarded by some historians as the distant ancestors of the "Houses of Trade" later established by the Iberian nations to control their colonial commerce in the sixteenth century.[8]

But these various Italian trading factories were not the only aspects of this imperial experience upon which Spain and Portugal were later to draw in creating their Atlantic empires. Within the Mediterranean area delimited by this network of factories, the cities of northern Italy soon elaborated an extensive commerce in many commodities, some of which were selected by historic circumstances to become the basic elements in the seaborne commerce of the Atlantic empires. Of these commodities, sugar, slaves, and gold illustrate particularly well the economic continu-ity between the medieval Mediterranean and the early Atlantic empires.

THE SUGAR TRADE

Long considered one of the more exotic spices, sugar arrived in the Mediterranean world along with the Arabic invaders of the seventh century. Although sugar never attained much of a market in the poor and backward West during the early Middle Ages, the situation gradually changed in the course of the twelfth century as returning crusaders popularized its use. Responding to this growth in demand, Italian merchants encouraged sugar cane planting in the Levant. Venetian investors, for example, set up cane fields in Tyre, and several of the crusading orders, such as the Hospitallers and the Teutonic Knights, initiated large-scale production on their estates. The product was then sold to Genoese merchants for final distribution in the West.[9]

As political instability in the Levantine area increased

---

[8] Charles Verlinden, *Précédents mediévaux de la colonisation en Amérique* (Mexico City, 1954), p. 20.

[9] *Ibid.,* pp. 46–48.

during the thirteenth century, and as the regular supply of the valuable commodity was jeopardized, Genoese merchants encouraged the development of other centers of production. With this development sugar began the slow migration westward, which ceased only when it had reached the islands of the Caribbean and the shores of Brazil early in the sixteenth century. Cane planting was first shifted to the island of Cyprus, which remained under Christian control throughout the later Middle Ages. Here we know that planters employing large numbers of Arabic slaves developed new methods of pressing the syrup from the cane through the use of water-driven engines. Somewhat later another center of production was brought to life by the Genoese in Sicily, but when political problems also disrupted supplies here, they began to look farther west for more stable areas of production.[1] In 1404 a Genoese merchant, Giovanni della Palma, introduced sugar cultivation into southern Portugal (Algarve); from there cultivation spread to the Madeira and Canary islands shortly after their settlement in the early fifteenth century. In Selection 3, Virgínia Rau provides a detailed description of the methods employed in sugar cane cultivation on Madeira at this time, as well as showing the deep involvement of various Genoese merchant families—the Spinola, the Lomellini, and the Doria—in its production and marketing. A similar economic situation developed on the Canary Islands, which were under the control of Castile, though production here was probably not as great as on Madeira.

From these island stepping stones sugar was introduced into Brazil and the Caribbean early in the sixteenth century. In both areas, Genoese merchants were deeply involved and thus continued in their role of spreading the cultivation of sugar cane to the areas of lowest cost of

---

[1] Carmelo Trasselli, "Produzione e commercio delle zucchero in Sicilia dal XIII al XIX sècolo," *Economia e Storia,* II (1955), 325–343.

production and greatest stability, which they first undertook, more than two centuries before, with the shift from Palestine to Cyprus.

THE SLAVE TRADE

The spread of sugar cultivation about the medieval Mediterranean was followed, like a parasite, by a trade in slaves who provided the necessary labor force for the plantations. Contrary to popular belief, the fall of the Roman Empire did not bring about the end of slavery in Europe. Throughout the Middle Ages a steady traffic in human beings was carried on, especially in the Mediterranean, where captured Muslims were sold to Christians and vice versa. During the centuries of reconquest, slave ranks in Christian Spain and Portugal were filled by Moors taken captive in border raids; few of the town charters of the period neglect to mention the prices and taxes which were levied on these slaves or *moros,* as they were called. But as the frontier moved southward, and finally vanished, this source eventually dried up. While the kingdoms of the Aragonese Confederation (Aragon, Valencia, and Catalonia) responded by turning eastward, to the Levant, for replacements, the kingdoms in the west, Portugal and Castile, found it more economical to import Negro slaves from North Africa. Brought up from the interior along with gold and ivory, they were offered for sale in the numerous small coastal ports of Morocco and Algeria.[2]

Somewhat later, with the discovery of the Canary Islands, another source was tapped. The primitive inhabitants of the islands, known as Guanches, were systematically hunted and carried back to Spain as slaves. But when the Castilian crown finally asserted its full authority over these islands, it discouraged further enslavement since it hoped to convert the natives to Christianity. Unfortunately

---

[2] Charles Verlinden, "Précédents et parallèles européens de l'esclavage colonial," *O Instituto*, CXIII (1950), 113–153.

these good intentions came a bit late, for the previous decades of unrestrained slaving had already effectively wiped them out.[3]

As the supply from the islands dwindled and prices in the Moroccan markets began to rise in consequence, enterprising noblemen-merchants of Portugal were encouraged to seek another source of supply along the Atlantic shore of Africa. By about the middle of the fifteenth century, some 2,500 slaves a year on the average were being brought back from this area to Portugal by expeditions (*resgates*) that bartered European trinkets for the "black ivory" which the Guinean litoral provided in such abundance. In fact the possibilities of this trade seemed so lucrative that in 1482 a Florentine investor, Bartolomeo Marchione, bought the *asiento* or monopoly franchise from the Portuguese king for more than 3 million reis a year. But when his profits proved to be even larger than he had imagined, the envious king promptly cancelled the contract and made the lucrative trade a royal monopoly, establishing special royal "Slave Houses" (*Casas de Escravos*) at Lisbon and Lagos for their sale.[4] Thus at the time of Columbus, a widespread and long-standing social pattern of slavery existed in the Iberian area. In Selection 4, Ruth Pike describes the slave caste of Seville at the time of the discoveries.

THE QUEST FOR GOLD

Along with slaves, the camel caravans which plodded up from the interior of Africa to the ports along the coast brought with them another commodity vital to the medi-

---

[3] D. J. Wölfel, "La curia Romana y la corona de España en la defensa de los aborígenes canários," *Anthropos*, XXV (1930), 1051–1065; Manuela Marrero Rodríguez, *La esclavitud en Tenerife a raíz de la Conquista* (La Laguna, 1966), pp. 13–40, 107–111.

[4] Vitorino Magalhães Godinho, *A economía dos descobrimentos henriquinos* (Lisbon, 1962), pp. 187–210.

eval Mediterranean economy: gold. During the early Middle Ages, most of the metal from the mines of central Africa had flowed across the Straits of Gibraltar into the *taifa* kingdoms of southern Spain, where it permitted them to maintain a gold coinage while the rest of Europe had to make do with silver. Thus supplied, these kingdoms developed a reputation for wealth which particularly excited the cupidity of the *reconquistadores*. As the "Poem of the Cid" remarks, "They have so much gold that they know not what to do with it."

With the increasing scope and intensity of Mediterranean commerce during the twelfth and thirteenth centuries, demand for gold as a medium of exchange grew apace. By the middle of the thirteenth century, several of the Italian cities had begun to mint gold coins, and their merchants increasingly frequented the ports of Muslim Spain and North Africa to purchase the yellow metal that the functioning of their far-flung trade interest required. By the fifteenth century, this demand had reached critical proportions, and the fact that Morocco and Granada were almost the only sources made this area a veritable focal point for trade in the western Mediterranean. From the *taifa* kingdom of Granada through which most of this gold flowed, the largest portion was taken out by Genoese merchants in payment for the manufactured goods that the small Muslim state imported.[5] The rest tended to be siphoned off by Castile in payments called *parias*, a sort of institutionalized blackmail, which the Granadine rulers periodically paid in return for a few more years of precarious independence.

But just as happened with the African slave trade, this flow of gold was disrupted about the middle of the fifteenth

---

[5] Federigo Melis, "Malaga nel sistema economico del XIV e XV sècolo," *Economia e Storia,* III (1956), 19–60; Jacques Heers, "Le Royaume de Grenade et la politique marchande de Gênes en Occident," *Le Moyen Âge,* LXIII (1957), 87–121.

century by Portuguese voyages down the Atlantic coast of
Africa, which put them in touch with the sources in the
Senegal river basin and along what soon became known as
the "Gold Coast." In thus tapping the supply directly, the
Portuguese ruined the Moroccan middlemen with their
camel caravans and collapsed the prosperity of the North
African ports. The first to suffer were Genoa and Castile
who had depended upon this flow for their metallic supplies. When this was choked off, they resorted to piratical
incursions against Portuguese shipping in the area and thus
forced the latter to apply to the Papacy for the first bulls of
extra-peninsular demarcation, prohibiting other nations
from entering "their" seas.

Outflanked by the Portuguese in the quest for precious
metals during the fifteenth century, the Castilians remedied
the situation with the discovery of the mines of Mexico
and Peru in the sixteenth. With the flow of precious metals
thus reestablished, the Castilian economy was enabled to
revert to the traditional system of "booty capitalism,"
which had begun with the looting of the *taifa* kingdoms
and the system of *parias* prevailing during the epoch of
reconquest.[6]

Shifting Focuses

Throughout the fourteenth century, Italian merchant
activities were concentrated in the East, while the western
Mediterranean remained a relatively underdeveloped back-
water. In the early fifteenth century, however, a series of
political developments greatly lessened the commercial
appeal of the East. The Sultan of Egypt raised the duties
that he levied on foreign traders, thus increasing the price
of the spices passing through his dominions; while the

---

[6] Ferdinand Braudel, "De l'or du Soudan a l'argent d'Amérique:
un drame méditerranéen," *Annales*: *Économies, Sociétés, Civil-
isations*, I (1946), 1–22.

Turks, who were gradually completing their conquest of the Black Sea region, soon deprived the Italians of the privileged status that they had been accustomed to enjoy as commercial parasites of the weakened Byzantine Empire. These blows, coming on top of the general trade recession that had been underway in Europe since the mid-fourteenth century, finally forced the Genoese to reorient their trade toward the previously neglected West. Here political conditions were more settled, a promising trade in gold and slaves was going on, and the expansion of the Castilian wool industry had made that kingdom into one of the richest markets of late medieval Europe.[7] In Selection 2, Charles Verlinden describes in detail this shift of Italian interest toward Iberia and its consequences for the age of exploration and discovery.

As might well be expected, Verlinden's emphasis on Italian involvement in the expansion of Iberia has provoked some patriotic, though not necessarily consistent, reaction from Iberian historians. Thus the Castilian medievalist, Claudio Sánchez-Albornoz reveals:

> I cannot follow Verlinden when he affirms that Genoese merchant quarters, factories, and trading concessions prefigure those which were created by the Spanish and the Portuguese. Some sort of filiation might be established between the colonial system of Portugal . . . [and] those which were used in the Mediterranean during the late Middle Ages. But there were enormous differences between the medieval colonization of the Genoese Republic, which had economic aims above all, and the bellicose and evangelistic colonization of Spain.[8]

This opinion forms an interesting contrast to that of the Portuguese historian of the discoveries, Vitorino Magalhães Godinho:

---

[7] Robert S. Lopez, "Market Expansion: the Case of Genoa," *Journal of Economic History,* XXIV (1964), 454–457.

[8] See Selection 1.

In the Spanish expansion foreign initiatives seem often to have played a decisive role, and frequently foreign capital was involved in it, while in the Portuguese expansion the initiatives seem almost always national.[9]

We shall deny ourselves the pleasure of arbitrating this dispute, which in any case involves factors which cannot be measured, and content ourselves instead with the question of the nature of the collaboration that developed between the Italians and the Iberians.

Here the decisive fact seems to be that by the fourteenth and fifteenth centuries, Italian businessmen had largely abandoned their previously active roles in trade and had turned to more sedentary occupations. As merchant-bankers they were interested in developing the economic potential of areas such as Portugal and Castile through investment of their surplus capital. Indeed, the nature of their interest in Iberian trade suggests parallels to the *commenda,* the classic business arrangement of the Mediterranean. In the *commenda,* most or all of the capital for a venture was put up by one partner who stayed home, while his associate undertook the active management of the voyage. Upon the latter's return the profits were split on some prearranged basis. Thus capital was wed to skill, and opportunities were offered to talent that might otherwise have been lost through lack of financing. Enlarging this metaphor to the late medieval Italo-Iberian relationship, one might liken the Genoese to the passive partner, the organizer and investor, while the Iberians assumed the role of active manager, supplying the bulk of the ships and the men who took the risk of far-flung voyages into the unknown.

Still, not all the investment in exploration was Italian; there were also Iberian entrepreneurs, usually nobles, even though their overall contribution was probably less important. Of them the best example, of course, is Henry the

---

[9] Godinho, *op. cit.,* p. 215.

Navigator himself—secretive, greedy, and celebate—whose devotion to profit would have warmed the heart of any bourgeois Calvinist. Just as many Italian nobles of the eleventh century shifted their capital from land to trade in order to profit from the higher rate of return, so Prince Henry mortgaged his estates to raise the capital necessary to finance his overseas trading ventures. Although the risk was great, the returns were higher still, and that was justification enough. Following his lead, other noblemen-merchants of Portugal, including the King himself, began to invest in a series of voyages down the coast of Africa in search of gold, pepper, and slaves—voyages which prepared the way for their successors who reached India and Brazil by the end of the century.

Italians, then, were not the only investors in discovery; neither were they the only sailors in the western Mediterranean. Their involvement, important as it was, should not obscure the contributions made by peninsulars themselves. In Portugal, long traditions of deep-sea fishing and coastal trading had produced a class of native mariners of considerable skill, who by the fifteenth century had become particularly active along the trade routes to northern Europe as well as in the Mediterranean.[1] In the latter area, it was Portuguese ships that dominated the transport of sugar from Madeira to the ports of Italy and even as far east as the island of Chios, the last surviving Genoese colony in the Levant. This involvement formed the prelude to the sugar trade of the Atlantic in the next century, when Brazilian and Caribbean production was carried back to Europe by Portuguese and Spanish ships sailing in the employ of Genoese and Dutch merchant distributors.

Equally involved in western Mediterranean trade during the fifteenth century were the Basques from the northern coast of Spain. They had begun by shipping wine, wool,

---

[1] Jacques Heers, "L'Expansion maritime portugaise à la fin du Moyen Âge: la Méditerranée," *Revista da Facultade de Letras de Lisbôa,* XXII (1966), 84–113.

and iron ore to northern Europe in the thirteenth and fourteenth centuries; by the fifteenth they had extended their activities into the Mediterranean where their political neutrality allowed them to render indispensable service in the carrying trade between Genoa and the Aragonese Empire.[2] The experience thus gained by the Basques well prepared them for the large role they were to play in the traffic of the Spanish Empire in America after 1500.

This presence of the Basques in the Mediterranean points up another important aspect of Iberian commerce on the eve of the discoveries—the eclipse of the Catalans. Latecomers to the trade of the Mediterranean, the Catalans had never been able to overtake the front-running Genoese and Venetians. Nevertheless, they enjoyed a burst of economic splendor during the century from 1250 to 1350. Because of their marginal position, however, they were particularly vulnerable to the economic contraction that set in during the second half of the fourteenth century. Unlike the Genoese who responded to the same contraction by reorienting their trade toward the West, the Catalans were blocked from such a solution not only by Portuguese and Castilian political hostility, but also by the growing conservatism of their merchant class. After a rash of bank failures in the late fourteenth century, the Barcelonese middle class tended to withdraw from speculative investments in trade and to put its money instead into rents and land. With a bourgeoisie so conservative, so adverse to risk and speculation, the Catalans in effect abandoned the field to the Genoese. Thus it was left to the latter to join with the Castilians and Portuguese in merchant ventures that discovered, first the islands of the Atlantic, and then the New World of America.[3]

Of this partnership, the archetypical example is, of course, Cristoforo Colombo. Too often, his career in the

---

[2] Jacques Heers, "Le Commerce des Basques en Méditerranée au XVe siècle," *Bulletin Hispanique,* LVII (1957), 292–324.
[3] Vicens Vives, *op. cit.,* pp. 211–214.

service of Castile, with its dramatic beginning and bitter ending, is presented in terms of personalities: an example of royal ingratitude to a devoted and visionary servant. Though these elements were certainly involved, the deeper reason for his unhappy fate lay far beyond the realm of personalities. For what happened to Columbus illustrates, in personal form, the intrinsic incompatibility of the two traditions that he attempted to harmonize; and his fate symbolizes the failure of the Italian and Iberian traditions to achieve the permanent amalgam that might have made the Iberian empires expressions of the most advanced elements in sixteenth-century European society, rather than of the most retrograde.

Trained as a seaman in the employ of Genoese merchants, Columbus conceived of the "Enterprise of the Indies" to which he devoted his mature years entirely in Mediterranean terms. By sailing west, this Marco Polo of the ocean sea hoped to reestablish contact with the fabulous East, which had been visited by Italian traders during the short-lived *Pax Mongolica* of the late thirteenth and fourteenth centuries.[4] But when he finally succeeded in reaching the Caribbean, and was confronted by a New World which he had not foreseen, difficulties set in. Obstinately holding to the idea that he was on the outskirts of China, he attempted to establish trading factories on the pattern of Genoese establishments in the Levant. Refusing to see the inappropriateness of his scheme to the realities of the area, he soon incurred the hostility of both his more pragmatic superiors and his more greedy subordinates, who resented his Mediterranean concepts and were simply eager to begin raiding the islands for slaves and searching for gold. Thus victimized by informers who denounced him to the Crown, and abandoned by his patrons who removed him for incompetence, Columbus soon found himself re-

---

[4] Samuel E. Morison, *Admiral of the Ocean Sea,* 2 vols. (Boston, 1942); Marianne Mahn-Lot, *Columbus* (New York, 1961).

placed by royal agents from Spain.[5] The latter promptly discarded his "Mediterranean" approach and proceeded instead to organize the islands after the Iberian tradition of conquest and settlement; in this fashion they paved the way for the conquest of the mainland and the establishment there of Castilian institutions of government and society.

Iberian Precedents: The Great Tradition

Once the seaways of empire had been traced out and a maritime bridge established, a culture and an ethos could be carried to the New World where they soon blended with indigenous elements to produce the variegated civilization of colonial Latin America. In attempting to describe the Iberian contribution to this amalgam, it will be helpful to employ a distinction proposed by the late Robert Redfield. Following his lead, we shall divide the culture that was brought across the Atlantic into a "Great Tradition," consisting of the legal concepts and governing institutions employed by the Crown to organize its dominion, and a "Little Tradition," composed largely of the habits, customs, and folkways, which had been elaborated over the centuries in the Iberian countryside.[6]

Fundamental to the Great Tradition were the medieval civil and religious concepts that provided the framework for the creation of the Spanish Empire. It was to this repertoire of doctrines elaborated by late medieval jurists that Castile looked for solutions to the problems that she faced concerning the legitimacy of her title to the Indies, the juridical status of the newly discovered territories in relation to the Crown, and, most important of all, the

---

[5] Richard Konetzke, *Entdecker und Eroberer Amerikas* (Frankfurt, 1963), pp. 12–26.

[6] Robert Redfield, *Peasant Society and Culture* (Chicago, 1956), pp. 40–59.

position that was to be accorded to the native Indian population within the framework of Castilian state and society.

In medieval Iberia, title to the lands taken from the Moors was derived from the fact of conquest, nicely legitimized and morally seconded by various papal declarations of crusade against the infidel. The defeated populations were considered to be without juridical rights, subject to the victor's will, and many of them were, in fact, enslaved. Because of this, hard-pressed Moorish kings sometimes hastened to surrender on the basis of treaties that ensured that the person, property, and religion of their subjects would be respected and that the inhabitants of their kingdoms would pass under the direct protection of the conquering ruler. In either case, however, title to the conquered territory derived from the act of conquest and was never considered to come from papal grant or proclamation of crusade. From time to time, it is true, peninsular rulers asked the Pope to adjudicate disputed territories between them; and the kings of Portugal and Aragon even enfeoffed their kingdoms to the Pope when diplomatic maneuvering made this advisable. But the latter was never allowed to claim overlordship in the newly acquired territories. These were regarded simply as *Hispania Irredenta*, lands that had originally pertained to Christian rulers, had subsequently been illegally occupied by heretic Muslims, and were in the process of being recovered.[7]

When the Iberian expansion was extended to overseas areas in the fifteenth century, peninsular rulers continued to apply reconquest precedents. Although Henry the Navigator attempted to reinforce his claim to the Canary Islands against Castile by securing papal assignment of the islands in 1434, when Castile and Portugal came to argue their respective claims before the Council at Basel in 1437, neither side invoked papal authority, but rather rested their

---

[7] Alfonso García Gallo, *Manual de história del derecho español*, 2 vols. (Madrid, 1959), I, 628–630.

arguments upon historical precedents interpreted in the light of Roman law.[8] In short, the Atlantic islands, North Africa, and later the New World were treated juridically in the same way as various parts of the peninsula had been previously; title was derived from discovery or conquest, and the Pope was appealed to merely as arbiter of overlapping claims.[9]

This practice of basing title upon conquest, however, soon broke down in America where an entirely new situation had to be faced. Unlike the peninsula or North Africa where it could be argued that Christian kings were merely recovering lands usurped by the Moors, in America there was a native population that had never heard of Christianity, could not long be confused with heretical Moors, and had never occupied lands that could be regarded as having once been Christian. Thus any decision concerning the legitimacy of Castile's title to America merged insensibly into questions about the status of the people who lived there and the proper relationship between them and the Christian world.

Here precedents were few. Medieval Europe's experience with non-Christians had been largely confined to Muslims who were more heretics than infidels. True, Italian traders like Marco Polo had visited the Far East in the early years of the fourteenth century, but the knowledge about these peoples which they disseminated was limited. Only in the New World was regular contact established between Europeans and peoples neither Christian nor Muslim. How were they to be treated, and what was to be their status and relationship vis-à-vis the Christian world?

Two traditions existed that could be drawn upon for answers. They might, for convenience, be designated the

---

[8] Luis Suárez Fernandez, *Relaciones entre Portugal y Castilla en la epoca del Infante Don Enrique, 1393–1460* (Madrid, 1960), pp. 244–272.

[9] Silvio Zavala, *Estúdios indianos* (Mexico City, 1948), pp. 7–15.

"conservative" and the "liberal." The conservative position received its classic formulation early in the thirteenth century by Cardinal Henry of Susa, usually referred to as *Hostiensis*. He argued that, since all human beings were first and foremost creatures of God, their right to possess property and to govern themselves was dependent upon divine grace. Since non-Christians, by definition, lacked this grace, they had no right to property and their governments were illegitimate. Therefore it was entirely proper for the Pope, as God's representative on earth, to distribute these peoples to suitable Christian princes for evangelization and governance as he saw fit.[1] This viewpoint remained dominant in canonical theory during most of the later Middle Ages and was still influential in the early sixteenth century when it was employed by certain lawyers to justify Castilian rule over the Indians in America. It ultimately became the basic argument used by *los Reyes Católicos* (the "Catholic Kings," as Ferdinand and Isabella were called) and occasionally even by their successors, to defend their rights in America against attack.

This doctrine of *Hostiensis,* however, had serious drawbacks, including the fact that it might be regarded as a tacit admission of papal overlordship in the Indies, something that Iberian rulers had been at extreme pains to avoid during the reconquest of the peninsula. Therefore Castilian rulers, by the time of Charles V, began to pay heed to another, more "liberal" point of view that denied any papal right to "grant" lands and people to anyone. This approach derived ultimately from the ideas of Aristotle, which had been reintroduced into European thought during the thirteenth century, and more directly from the synthesis of these ideas with Christian dogma that had been achieved by St. Thomas Aquinas. According to this tradition, property and self-government were not the result of grace, not a "gift of God," handed down from above, but rather the

---

1 Walter Ullmann, *A History of Political Thought: The Middle Ages* (Baltimore, 1965), p. 115.

natural response of men to their need to live together in society. Although non-Christian societies, argued St. Thomas, were imperfect in the sense that they did not know Christ, they nevertheless had as "natural" a right to property and self-government as did Christians.[2] And although this doctrine was not widely accepted during the later Middle Ages, it continued, nevertheless, to be championed by the Dominicans, St. Thomas' order, with whom it became a kind of intellectual tradition.

About the turn of the sixteenth century, two political theorists, Juan de Torquemada and Cardinal Cajetan, one Spanish, the other Italian, attempted a kind of synthesis of the two points of view. They distinguished between (1) those infidels who had deliberately rejected Christianity and were thus proper subjects of conquest for their contumacy; and (2) the innocent heathen who had never had an opportunity to know Christianity, and whose possessions and freedom were therefore to be respected. Thus, on the eve of the conquest of America, three different types of non-Christians were distinguished: first, there were Muslims who were considered incorrigible heretics and could with good conscience be enslaved; second, there were infidels who were not Muslims and who after converting to Christianity were to be confirmed in their freedom; and finally, those who had been offered the opportunity to convert, but had refused to do so, and were therefore to be equated with Muslims, conquered, and enslaved.[3]

The subsequent "struggle for justice," as Lewis Hanke has aptly called it, was essentially an attempt to adapt these medieval concepts to the infinite complexity of the Indian civilizations of America. Could war and conquest, in fact, be justified by the Indians' reluctance to convert? Did the necessity of conquest to compel conversion produce a legitimate title to the New World for Castile? And if the

---

[2] *Ibid.*, pp. 174–185; Thomas Aquinas, *Summa contra Gentiles*, II, 10.

[3] García Gallo, *op. cit.*, I, 629–630.

Indians were thus conquered, could they be enslaved in accordance with the Reconquest tradition? The answers to these questions varied depending upon time, place, and the people involved. All too often, the forcible solution won out. But one should not overlook the fact that the conflict also produced a theoretical synthesis that was, in fact, the beginning of the modern law of nations. Elaborated by the Spanish Dominican, Francisco de Vitoria, it represented a singular intellectual victory of the "liberal" Mediterranean tradition over the Iberian habit of conquest: the Indians, he maintained, were free men, constituting legitimate societies as St. Thomas had taught. And the only justification for the presence of Spaniards in their lands came, not from any right to conquer non-Christian peoples, but from the natural right of nations to engage in preaching the Gospel and to enter into mutually beneficial trade relationships with all nations of the world.[4]

Questions regarding the validity of their title to the Indies and their right to rule over the native population did not, however, deter the rulers of Castile from proceeding to organize their newly conquered territories on the pattern of the Crown of Castile. It is important to note that at the end of the fifteenth century, the Crown of Castile, unlike that of Aragon, was not a conglomeration of separate kingdoms each having its own law, tax, and administrative systems, but rather an integrated whole with a law and administration common to all its component regions. Nevertheless, the territory of the kingdom of Castile was considered by custom to be divided into two distinct categories. In certain areas the powers of lordship were exercised by nobles or institutions other than the king. Land under the control of monasteries was termed *abadengo;* if under the control of a noble it was called *señorío;* while land controlled by the military orders was usually termed an *encomienda.* Over the rest of the realm, the king himself was the immediate lord. This part of the kingdom was called *realengo;* and

---

[4] *Ibid.,* pp. 636–638.

here, in addition to his general supreme authority, the king also enjoyed extensive seignorial rights.[5]

During the Reconquest, the constant addition of new territory had been sufficient to replenish the *realengo,* and thus provide the fiscal basis for a strong monarchy.[6] But when the possibility of adding new land ceased with the end of the Reconquest, not only did the expansion of the *realengo* stop; it was soon depleted through grants that the rebellious nobility continually wrested by force from a weakened monarchy.

This depletion of the *realengo* was one of the principal problems with which Ferdinand and Isabella were struggling in their attempts to reestablish royal authority when the unforeseen discovery of America changed the situation dramatically. This windfall brought them not only a new *realengo* vast beyond imagination, but also a territory in which their powers were derived from conquest and in which there was no Spanish community that could claim rights as against those of the monarch. Once this vast territory was acquired, how did the rulers of Spain decide to administer their windfall? Theoretically, they were free to create whatever institutions they wished, since here their rights were untrammeled by the traditional privileges of the various classes and corporate bodies of medieval Spain. In fact, of course, they were bound by the traditions of their society and by the objective conditions which existed in the New World. What they set up was a government and administration much like what already existed in Castile, adapted and adjusted by trusted administrators on the spot to the realities of the new situation. Unfortunately the medieval origins of only a few of these institutions implanted in the New World have been studied, and for that reason no general synthesis or comment can be made. Two of the most important institutions, however, are dealt with

---

[5] Mário Góngora, *El estado en el derecho indiano* (Santiago, 1951), pp. 25–41.

[6] Sánchez-Albornoz, *op. cit.,* II, 510.

in the selections. Robert S. Chamberlain studies the medieval backgrounds of the *ecomienda* in Selection 6; while in Selection 7, John Preston Moore summarizes the structure of the medieval Castilian town.

Iberian Precedents: The Little Tradition

In contrast to the Great Tradition which arrived in the wake of the conquistadors and was often imposed by force of arms, the Little Tradition of popular culture was brought by the friars and insinuated into native life through the matrix of religion. It was only natural that the mendicant orders of Franciscans and Dominicans should take the lead in this work of evangelization. Since their foundation in the thirteenth century, their special task had been to revivify the faith through teaching and preaching among urban masses grown indifferent to the dogmas of Christianity. In performing this role, they rapidly developed a number of potent and aggressive techniques of persuasion based upon a sophisticated blend of rhetoric and reason. Thus prepared, they disdained to confine their activities to the Christian world. What was good for alienated Christians was even better for infidels. Soon friars were trying out their eloquence on the shores of Africa where a steady stream of them went out on peaceful crusades in quest of souls. And although their eloquence proved small defence in moments of crisis, and a goodly number suffered martyrdom for their presumption, the tendency to favor peaceful persuasion in the place of armed crusade grew stronger in the later Middle Ages and found particular favor with the mendicant orders.

In Iberia this tradition was brilliantly represented by Raymond Lull, the Catalan friar and philosopher who learned Arabic in order to win over his Muslim audiences by writing and preaching the Christian faith to them in their own tongue. As the foremost advocate of missionary activity among the infidel, he thrice crossed over to Africa before being stoned to death by an infuriated mob outside the city of Bougie in North Africa, where his body was recovered by Genoese merchants and brought back to Spain.

In spite of such inauspicious events, the ideas of Lull did not die out; and alongside the advocates of the older ideas of crusade and conquest, there were always Iberian friars who exemplified the way of persuasion. As Kubler shows in Selection 8, the experience that these friars gained in preaching among the peasantry of Extremadura and Andalusia, as well as among the Muslims of Granada after its conquest, well prepared them for their saintly apostolate to the Indies. After the administrative reform of their orders in the reign of Ferdinand and Isabella, and after the later addition of Erasmian doctrines of humanism and tolerance, they were well equipped to accomplish the lasting achievement which Robert Ricard calls the "spiritual conquest" of America.[7]

Most of the Little Tradition that the friars transmitted to the Indians had been absorbed in the villages and countryside of southwestern Spain, where these culture traits were inextricably mingled and permeated with religious significance. Carried to the New World, this popular culture was communicated to the Indians through the constant contact that the friars maintained with them in the "reductions" and congregations organized to indoctrinate them with Christianity. In these communities, whose very creation had the effect of disorganizing the older native traditions, the Indians learned, inseparably from the faith, the Castilian language and the Spanish ceremonies of life, as well as Spanish arts, crafts, and agricultural practices.

In seeking to determine what influence the Little Tradition of Iberia had on native life in America, George Foster, an anthropologist, has done important research in comparing the various elements of Spain's rural culture with those

---

[7] Robert Ricard, *La Conquête spirituelle du Méxique* (Paris, 1933).

of the New World. In Mexico he has discovered widespread existence of traditional Spanish plows and water wheels, weaving techniques and potter's kilns, wool clothing, wheeled carts and sledges, as well as legal customs of equal inheritance among children that were unknown to the indigenous societies. The origin of nearly all of these traits can be traced to the southwestern part of Spain.[8] This tends to confirm the conclusions reached by other scholars, working from other types of evidence, that the majority of the early migrants to America came from the province of Extremadura and from the region about Seville.[9]

Nothing as detailed and thorough as the work of Foster has been done with respect to the transmission of Portuguese culture to Brazil. Nevertheless, Gilberto Freyre and Emilio Willems have studied "The Portuguese Colonizer"[1] and "Portuguese Culture in Brazil,"[2] respectively, but their comments do not go much beyond intuitive generalizations, often of a fanciful character. On the other hand, Orlando Ribeiro, a cultural geographer, has shrewdly analyzed the early patterns of settlement in the Madeira Islands and concludes that the first wave of Portuguese to venture overseas came from the south of the country (the Algarve). Only later, during the settlement process in Brazil, did the source of emigrants shift to the north of Portugal, to the heavily populated Minho region, which furnished the majority of the Portuguese who went abroad thereafter.[3] As with the Castilians, the culture that these

---

[8] George Foster, *Culture and Conquest* (New York, 1960).

[9] Peter Boyd-Bowman, "Regional Origins of the Earliest Spanish Colonists of America," *PMLA,* LXXI (1956), 1152–1172.

[1] Gilberto Freyre, *The Masters and the Slaves,* Samuel Putnam (tr.) (New York, 1961), pp. 4–14.

[2] Emilio Willems, "Portuguese Culture in Brazil," *Proceedings of the International Colloquium on Luso-Brazilian Studies* (Nashville, Tenn., 1953), pp. 66–78.

[3] Orlando Ribeiro, *Aspectos e problemas da expansão portuguêsa* (Lisbon, 1962), pp. 22–26.

Portuguese took with them was largely blended into a religious matrix as Jaime Cortesão emphasizes in Selection 10.

In all these cases, the Little Tradition, unlike the Great, had to make its way into ground that was already occupied, so to speak, by a native culture that remained relatively intact even after the collapse of the Indian political superstructure. This Iberian culture could enter only here and there, through the fractures which opened up as the native religious organizations disintegrated. Ironically enough, this "incomplete" victory in the countryside was to prove more lasting than the more dramatic change of political power, for instead of a pattern artificially imposed from above, there was created an authentic blend of Iberian and Indian that remains even today the most significant and lasting influence that Iberia exerted upon the various New World societies that it discovered and conquered.

Problems for Solution

Some fifteen years ago Charles Verlinden, in concluding his essay on medieval precedents for American colonization, suggested a number of themes for research in the field.[4] Unhappily, few of his suggestions have been taken up in the intervening years, a lack of response which well indicates both the neglect from which the field has suffered as well as the varied preparation necessary for work in it. An exception to this lack of response has been Professor Ruth Pike of Hunter College, whose recent study of the Genoese in Seville and their participation in the financing and organizing of the various voyages to America shows what can be done by a person with the requisite training.[5] But we still need to know much more about Genoese in-

---

[4] Verlinden, *Précédents mediévaux de la colonisation en Amérique, op. cit.,* pp. 60–61.

[5] Ruth Pike, *The Genoese in Seville and the Opening of the New World* (Ithaca, 1956).

volvement and about the interrelationships between Iberian enterprise and European capital in organizing the early voyages of discovery. As yet only the surface of the subject has been scratched.

We also need more detailed knowledge of the processes of reconquest and settlement in medieval Iberia: how the conquered land was distributed and to what extent the Muslim communities were integrated, socially, economically, and politically, into the Christian kingdoms. Robert I. Burns' recent study of the reconquest of Valencia is a model on these matters, but unfortunately it deals with an area of the peninsula that had little influence (as far as we know) on American conquest and settlement.[6] Júlio González's work on the settlement of Seville is replete with information, but he is unfortunately not concerned with possible precedents for overseas colonization.[7]

A particularly rich field of inquiry, still virtually untouched, relates to the civil and canonistic background to the "struggle for justice" in the Indies and to medieval views concerning the respective juridical rights of infidels and heretics. A few monographs have sketched out parts of the subject, but no comprehensive synthesis has yet been attempted.[8]

Another flagrant lacuna appears in the matter of late medieval Iberian institutional history, a lack unfortunately but unavoidably reflected both in the Introduction and in the selections of the present volume. To what extent were the viceregal offices, the *cabildos,* and *audiencias* of America faithful copies of their Iberian parent institutions? To

---

[6] Robert I. Burns, S.J., *The Crusader Kingdom of Valencia; Reconstruction on a Thirteenth-Century Frontier,* 2 vols. (Cambridge, 1967).

[7] González, *op. cit.*

[8] Venáncio D. Carro, O.P., "Las controversias de Indias y las ideas teológico-jurídicas medievales que las preparan y explican," *Anuário de la Asociatión Francisco de Vitoria,* XX (1948), 13–53; Paulino Castañeda Delgado, *La teocracía pontifical y la conquista de América* (Vitoria, 1958).

what extent was old form infused with new meaning and function in the new social environment? The disappearance of the Castilian royal chancery has hampered such studies, but the remaining documentation could tell us much if it were systematically explored. Recently García de Valdeavellano[9] has given us an excellent introduction to the subject, but details and nuances are lacking. Only when we fully understand the constitutional development of late medieval Spain can we really begin to assess whether Castilian and Portuguese colonial institutions represented a traditional conservative response, or were, in reality, innovations in the face of a new situation.

Finally, possibly the most important question of all still remains to be answered. What was it that happened in European society during the fourteenth and fifteenth centuries that impelled it to embark upon an expansion greater and more aggressive than anything previously experienced in world history? And why were the Iberian nations the chosen agents of destiny for its realization? The answers to these related questions must certainly involve the "shifting of gears" in the European economy, which occurred after the mid-fourteenth century and which is still the subject of much controversy. While Marxist historians wish to see the genesis of European expansion as the work of a bourgeoisie which had accumulated the necessary capital through increased exploitations of the peasantry, their neo-Malthusian opponents insist that it was the reduction of Europe's population during the plagues of the fourteenth century that freed the capital resources required for the risky investments leading to the attainment of India and the discovery of America.[1]

But along with this question regarding the manner in

---

[9] Luis García de Valdeavellano, *Curso de Historia de las Instituciones Españolas* (Madrid, 1968).
[1] Michel Mollat, *et al.,* "L'économie européenne au deux derniers siècles du Moyen Age," *Relazioni del X Congresso Internazionale di Scienze Storiche* III (Florence, 1955), 655–811.

which the necessary capital for exploration and discovery was accumulated, there is finally the question of the imagination. Here, in the hopes and visions of a figure like Columbus, may rest the deeper explanation of the Iberian expansion; for without the idea of linking Europe by sea with the Far East, of encompassing all mankind into one known world, the capital accumulated by Europeans would have lain inert or have been devoted to luxury expenditures. In this sense "one world" had to be imagined before it could be realized. And thus, in addition to the progress of rational calculation, which Max Weber sees as the most significant development in European civilization during the late Renaissance and Reformation, one must reckon with the dimension of the irrational—of the mystical-religious imaginings of men like Columbus with his plan of attaining the East by sailing West, of finding the earthly paradise, and of fulfilling the Pauline dream and Biblical prophecies by spreading the Gospel to the entire human race.[2] For these were among the crucial concepts that brought about, not merely the emergence of modern Europe, but the incomparably more significant result of a global civilization, the creation of one world of which the Iberian conquest and settlement of Latin America was the first act.

[2] Mahn-Lot, *op. cit.*, pp. 54–59, 156–160.

ONE

❀

FROM MEDIEVAL
TO MODERN
COLONIZATION

1

CLAUDIO SÁNCHEZ-ALBORNOZ

THE CONTINUING TRADITION OF RECONQUEST

During its formative stages, the empire that Castile constructed in the New World was in many respects a trans-Atlantic revival, with variations, of the medieval experience of reconquest. This "prolongation" of the Spanish Middle Ages into America, with its frontier warfare, its spirit of crusade, its anachronistic mores and ethos, helps to explain many characteristics of colonial Latin American life. Equally significant, the prolongation and reinforcement of these characteristics in the Spanish Empire tended to retard the normal development of the metropolis itself, as Sánchez-Albornoz points out in the following selection, and thus contributed to the "decline of Spain," which has attracted the perennial attention of historians, economists, and essayists.

Don Claudio Sánchez-Albornoz was born in the Castilian town of Ávila in 1893 and began his lifelong study of medieval Spain as a pupil of the great social

From Claudio Sánchez-Albornoz, *España, un enigma histórico*, 2 vols. (Buenos Aires: Editorial Sudamericana, 1956), II, excerpted from pp. 500–513. Translated and printed by permission of Editorial Sudamericana.

*and legal historian, Eduardo de Hinojosa. In addition
to pursuing his career as an historian, he became
Rector of the University of Madrid in 1924 and was
later named Ambassador to Portugal by the government of the Spanish Republic. After the Civil War
and the rise of Franco, he went into voluntary exile in
Buenos Aires, where he now heads the Instituto de
História de España and edits the journal,* Cuadernos
de história de España. *Among his many significant
contributions to Spanish history are* Estampas de la
vida en León hace mil años, En torno a los orígines del
feudalismo, Instituciones medievales españolas, *and
his interpretative work,* España, un enigma histórico,
from which this selection has been taken.

No one disputes, nor can dispute, the fact that the discovery and settlement of America has been the great
historic achievement of the Iberian peoples. None of Hispania's other contributions to human history can be compared to it. It is enough to repay all the debts that Spain
may owe to Europe and to counterbalance all the contributions made by other nations to Western culture. We
created the boundaries of the Western world itself, of
which the Atlantic today is the interior sea, and we
provoked the greatest shock ever experienced by the Old
World, confined for centuries to the Mediterranean by the
waves of the Atlantic. Neither the intellectual revolutions
of the Renaissance and the Reformation, creations of Italy
and Germany, nor the scientific achievements of the other
nations north of the Pyrenees surpass the great Hispanic
enterprise in historic consequences. Because we incorporated America into Western life, modern scientific and
technical knowledge came to rapid maturity . . . and
modern capitalism could take shape thanks to the gold that
was brought from across the Atlantic: science, technical

knowledge, and capitalism without whose coming together the industrial transformation of Europe would have been impossible.

.   .   .

But I think in this way, no one can accuse me of disdain for our marvelous American adventure, nor place me among those who argue about the material or spiritual damage that it may have brought to Spain. . . . But in judging the magnitude of the Spanish enterprise in America I do not always hold that all of its effects on the Spanish way of life were favorable.

Twenty five years ago . . . I presented the theory that the Spanish conquest of America had been a projection of the Spanish Middle Ages in space and in time, and I ventured the thesis that it had prolonged the medieval character of Spain itself. For how can the conquest of America possibly be seen as anything but the most immense result of the peninsular activism created by Spain's centuries-long struggle with Islam? How can one not see in the discovery and conquest of America the last heroic age of the western world, the last phase of the medieval epic? When Spanish activity in America is compared with that of other European peoples, does not Spanish medievalism—part crusade and part adventure—stand out as clear as day?

Unlike the Roman conquest of the West, which was planned, directed, and realized by the state, Spain's conquest of America revealed the dispersed and disordered action of the Castilian people, deprived of the effective guidance of its governing elite, almost abandoned by the Spanish monarchy, and led by a foreign dynasty into enterprises alien to its interests. And how, under such conditions, could a nonmedieval nation, a nation subjected to the rigid articulations of an ancient or modern state, have been able to realize such an enterprise? How can one not see in that activity, so filled with individualism, the imprint of medieval life and society, in which the hero, the personal and isolated effort, acted with the greatest freedom and achieved the most immense results in peace and in war?

.　.　.

"At the beginning of the Modern Age," I wrote many years ago, "any European people would have had to improvise a policy of colonization if it had discovered America. Any, that is, except Spain, rich in the experience of conquest and colonization; for no other people of the West had had the opportunity to undergo a similar preparation." I continue to think the same today. The great Belgian historian, [Charles] Verlinden, has exaggerated the influence on Spanish colonization of the colonial traditions of the Italian *signorias* in the Mediterranean. . . . I cannot follow Verlinden when he affirms that Genoese merchant quarters, factories, and trading concessions prefigure those which were created by the Spanish and the Portuguese. Some sort of filiation might be established between the colonial system of Portugal—and also of Holland, which later followed in the Portuguese wake—with that which was used in the Mediterranean during the late Middle Ages. But there were enormous differences between the medieval colonization of the Genoese Republic, which had economic aims above all, and the bellicose and evangelistic colonization of Spain.

The conquest of the great American empire, inhabited by idolatrous peoples with barbarous customs; the diffusion of Spanish faith, culture, law, and way of life throughout an immense continent; and the juridical articulation of these lands gained by the sword into the mechanism of the Castilian state have no possible parallel in the traditional methods of colonization of the Genoese *signoria*. The presence in Andalusia of a group of Genoese navigators and bankers, as well as the rare trips made by some of them to the Indies, did not exert any notable influence on the imperial colonies of Spain. The mercantile spirit, the taste for business, and the dreams of commercial gain carried little weight with them. To the possible detriment of their own imperial activity, with its seignorial and religious character, the Castilians neither learned nor tried to learn anything fundamental from the Genoese colonial system.

Verlinden recognizes that the capitulations drawn up by Columbus with Ferdinand and Isabella and the privileges which he obtained from them after his discoveries were rooted in the pure medieval Castilian tradition. And if the Genoese played a role (a role that was really less than minimal) in the first days of Caribbean exploration, the Hispanic venture soon took a direction that was entirely unconnected with medieval Italian colonization. There are, in fact, much greater differences between the Hispanic colonial techniques of the sixteenth through the eighteenth centuries . . . and European colonial enterprise of the nineteenth and twentieth centuries. The latter was the result of economic imperialism, product of the contemporary industrial revolution, which the great Belgian historian correctly distinguishes from the Hispano-Atlantic tradition. But the colonial creations of Spain in America, which were organs of power rather than economic centers, were rooted in the peninsula's medieval history.

.   .   .

"Each day it becomes increasingly clear that the whole history of medieval Castile is resumed and crystalized in an uninterrupted and gigantic enterprise of colonization," I wrote in 1930; and I continue to believe the same today. From the eighth century on, the history of Spanish Christendom is, in effect, the history of a slow but continuous restoration of Spain as an integral part of Europe; and the history of Castile, that of the constant advance of a small kingdom . . . which expanded from the mountain peaks and thickets of Asturias until it reached the blue and luminous sea to the south—the history of a people's hard-won expansion into the sunny land of Andalusia. In the wake of hard-fought battles, the Castilians spread over the plains, crept over the hills, and filed across the mountains that stood in their path—and kept on fighting and settling through space and time. Just as later in America, these eight medieval centuries[1] were a complex succession of conquests, the founding of cities, the establishment of episcopal sees and monasteries, the creation of institutions of war and of government, the mixture of cultures and peoples—in short, the transplantation of a race and a language, of a faith and a civilization.

"Although the characteristics diverged depending upon the epoch in which it occurred, each advance, from the first under the kings of Asturias to the last under the reunited crowns of Aragon and Castile, always involved a permanent colonizing activity, always carried toward the south the language born in the valleys of northern Castile, always propagated the teachings of Christ in the territory won by the sword, always installed in the new domains the peculiar ways of life that Castile's own history had been creating, always extended toward the south the municipal liberties that had arisen in the Duero valley, and always incorporated new kingdoms into the state that Castile, as the heir of classical antiquity and the Visigothic tradition, was forging bit by bit during its struggle over the centuries with Islam."

Then when the Reconquest ended and it seemed as if Castile's colonizing activity had come to an end with the attainment of the Atlantic-Mediterranean sea barrier, the naval tradition (already two centuries old) made it possible for Columbus to discover America the unknown. The bellicose energies of the impetuous Castilians were channeled into the new adventure, still unsurpassed by modern man, of the conquest of the Indies. There across the sea, Castile's medieval history was repeated and the destiny of

---

[1] The author is thinking of a period extending roughly from 711 (the date of the Moorish invasion of Spain) to 1492 (the date of the reconquest of Granada). In a more limited sense, the *Reconquista* lasted from circa 850 to 1250. See the Introduction. (Ed.)

Castile fulfilled once again. The scenery was not the same, and neither were the characteristics of her colonization, just as they had not been the same in Spain throughout the centuries. The plains, which lie to the north of the Duero river, had been populated by small freeholders, by minor nobles, and by monasteries from 850 on; great town councils brought back to life the zone between the Duero and the Tagus rivers after the conquest of Toledo (1085); the military orders accomplished the repopulation of Extremadura and La Mancha after the victory of Las Navas de Tolosa (1213); municipalities and magnates colonized lower Andalusia after the conquest of Seville (1248) . . . with each advance of the frontier new methods of colonization were applied, but the enterprise was always undertaken in the same spirit of crusade and plunder, with the cross held high and one's pockets empty, with the same greed for riches and for the conversion of souls, and with the same traditions of Western liberty and civilization carried on the points of swords and lances.

Just as Spain had acted as the vanguard of the West in the face of crude, barbarous Africa during the Middle Ages, so she later was the forerunner of Europe facing a new world on American soil. Just as the ordinary peasants came down from the mountains of Asturias and Cantabria to the plains of the Duero valley greedy for liberty and riches, or the poorer nobility hungry for fortune and glory, so the penniless hidalgos and plebian adventurers embarked for America seven centuries later. Just as the monastic foundations . . . brought great depopulated areas back to life in Spain before the year 1000, so the Castilian religious missions contributed to the colonization of the American continent after 1500. And just as the colonists of the frontier in Spain near the Muslim fortresses were granted lands and liberty, so privileges and *repartimientos* (grants of Indian labor) were given to the Spanish vanguard in the new continent.

The egalitarian and integrationist policy of Castile, unique in the history of world colonization, a policy that did not treat the conquered lands as colonies but considered them simply as a prolongation of the national territory, was rooted in the oldest Castilian traditions. As they conquered diverse Muslim kingdoms, from Toledo to Granada, century after century, the kings of Asturias, León, and Castile incorporated and assimilated them on an equal footing with their own kingdoms. How can one not see in the recognition of the Indians as Castilian citizens the logical projection of the juridical doctrines of Castile in its peninsular undertakings: a Castile that had also made the conquered Moors into citizens?

We discovered, conquered, and colonized America in accordance with our medieval experience. We did not have to improvise a policy of expansion and colonization, for we continued seven centuries of peninsular history across the Atlantic. Behind the astonishing events of exploration, the titanic work of conquest, and the fruitful days of colonial settlement, a new Spain rose up between the Atlantic and the Pacific. . . . Thus we overcame the tradition of many thousands of years that had linked the development of ancient civilizations to the shores of the Mediterranean and that confined Western culture to the narrow limits of Europe. As I said at the beginning of this essay, no historic undertaking among those which contributed to the birth of the modern world had greater consequences than the American adventure. Neither the Renaissance nor the Reformation equaled its burden of decisive influences in the future of man. . . . The collaboration of Spain in creating the modern world was not inferior to any other people of the West. But, without any risk of paradox, one may also say that with the birth overseas of a new world and a new Spain, and indeed as a result of its own creation, the old Spain that had been reborn in Europe a short while before was weakened and finally destroyed. . . .

The American undertaking confirmed the providential conception of life that was already traditional among the Spanish. Aside from the incarnation and death of Christ, they regarded the discovery of the Indies as the greatest event that had occurred since the creation of the world. Las Casas considered Columbus as the Elect of God, designated for the accomplishment of this great task. "The conquest of the Indies began when that of the Moors was over," wrote López de Gómara, "for the Spanish have always fought against infidels." They were the instrument of the Most High for the incorporation of the latter into the Mystic Body of Our Lord through the reception of the gospel from Spanish lips. The discovery and conquest were brought to a conclusion by the goodness of the Lord so that Spain, called to be the champion of the faith in Europe, could increase its power and wealth. Even men of science such as Acosta . . . whose doctrines prepared the way for the philosophy of unlimited progress, believe in the providential of the great adventure.

For the Spanish, these ideas . . . affirmed their old beliefs about the continual intervention of the Divine in the life of those below and about the continued action of Eternal God in their favor as a reward for their warlike, divine activities. And these ideas contributed to keeping alive their servile religiosity. "I serve you, therefore you owe me protection," was how these men who fought against the idolatrous Indians of America continued to think as they addressed themselves to God, in a prayer at once arrogant and presumptuous. . . .

When the frontier in Spain was closed and the clergy could no longer expand and enrich itself with lands taken from the Moors, there opened up on the other side of the Atlantic a virgin world for the diffusion and spread of the Church. In this way the Spanish church was able to replace . . . its mission with respect to the Muslims by the imperious necessity of work in America. And this activity across the sea was of great help in preserving its traditional economic power and in safeguarding its great influence within the Spanish state and society.

The expansion of the Spanish Empire in America, far from changing the equilibrium of political forces in Spain, strengthened it for several centuries more. If the medieval monarchs, by successive advances and repeated colonizations, had been able to replenish their income, which slowly diminished during the periods when the frontier was stable, so the Spanish crown accomplished similar restoration of its treasure with the riches that the galleons and fleets brought back from the Indies. If the kings of Castile, in conquering and colonizing the zones gained from the Caliphate or from the *taifa* kings, from the Almohad empire or from Granada, had reaped a copious booty of lands and offices with which to attract and dominate both nobles and ordinary people, so the Spanish sovereigns found, in the viceroyalties, captaincies, *audiencias, corregimientos,* and *cabildos* overseas, a vast treasure of bureaucratic gifts, posts from high to low, with which to continue to attract the importunate aristocratic minorities, as well as the masses of the people, to revolve like stars around them.

The conquest and colonization of Spain contributed in a decisive way to strengthening the juridical power of the Castilian monarchy; and our action in America, in modern times, contributed no less to the omnipotence of the Spanish kingship. By the sixteenth century, the old Castilian liberties were dead. Only the legalistic spirit of Philip II's reign permitted some vitality to the ancient Cortes of Castile. But American gold also cooperated in killing and burying these liberties and in impeding their resurrection. If the Spanish monarchy had not been able to rely on the resources of America during the seventeenth and eighteenth centuries, would it have been able to remain so strong? Would it not have encountered difficulties similar to those which led to the French and English revolutions [against the crown]? If the fleets of America had not partially supplied the necessities of the treasury, would not the pressure of taxation have raised up the masses against [the monarchy]?

The reinforcement of the monarchy's political power through the American adventure contributed to make the traditional Spanish equation between power, wealth, and service a permanent one. The spreading national bureaucracy found in America a magnificent place to take root and fabulously expand. Throngs of Spaniards who had obtained royal nominations or who were in the service of Viceroys, *Adelantados,* or Captains General crossed the Atlantic, . . . thousands of *peninsulares* . . . dreamed of a post on the other side of the Atlantic. And many of them realized their dreams. [Across the Atlantic] went members of famous families (many Borgias, for example, lived in Peru), many hidalgos without means, and penniless soldiers. When the central organs of the metropolitan government for the Indies denied Cervantes' request for a post in the Indies, they unconsciously made possible the marvelous brilliance of *Don Quixote de La Mancha,* which would certainly never have been written in Guatemala. . . . How many other sharp minds, how many businessmen, how many human values were lost to the Spanish people in the security of the bureaucratic life in the Indies!

In Spanish economic life, the conquest and colonization of America also accentuated, in a manner already well-known, the fatal consequences that had already been present in the conquest and colonization of medieval Spain. The centuries of war against the Muslims and Africans, and the resulting territorial gains, drew the most daring and bravest men away from industrial and commercial activities; the discovery, the conquest, and the exploration of America was equally influential in removing many open minds and ambitious wills from economic enterprise. The hope for riches, which could be had from the conquest of infidel kingdoms, impelled the men of Castile toward the exercise of arms, in which one could easily prosper as the frontier advanced into Muslim territory; but in the same way the fantastic dream of fabulous gains in the rich provinces of America pulled thousands and thousands of Spaniards away from peaceful tasks in the peninsula to hurl them into overseas adventure. The territorial and bureaucratic booty that each new thrust of Christianity into Saracen lands put into the hands of kings and, through them, into the control of the *conquistadores,* converted many peasants, artisans, and merchants of Castile into warriors and thus separated the whole of the Castilian lower nobility from peaceful occupations. The enormous abundance of lands and offices of every sort, which the political organization of the Indies was creating, thrust a multitude of active and peaceful Spaniards, who otherwise would have pursued their economic labors in Spain, from their fields and shops into overseas exploits, toward the bureaucracy and wealth of America. . . .

And as has already been said, the attraction that America exerted on the rising industry of Castile was so great that the latter was unable to develop naturally. The rising demand for merchandize, which came to Castile from the Indies, ended by gravely damaging the development of Castilian industrial capacity. In only a few decades, the acquisitive power of the Spaniard who crossed the Atlantic was augmented fabulously and the vast native masses were converted into customers of the peninsular artisans. To fulfill such orders [from the New World], [Spain] resorted to the purchase of foreign goods. Thus was perpetuated the *ancien lien* that foreign industry had kept on our national wealth for centuries. This competition of foreign goods was facilitated and favored by the businessmen who traded in the south of the peninsula. The wave of precious metals, which arrived from America onto Spanish shores, by initiating a revolution in prices, altered the cost of living and the value of wage labor in Spain before it did so across the Pyrenees, and foreign industries could sell more cheaply than Castile the products so urgently solicited by the markets of the Indies. In the face of this series of adverse circumstances, Spanish and foreign merchants increasingly gave a greater place to non-Spanish goods in the trade with America. And this, then, is how the great American undertaking finally came, by another route, to be an obstacle to the economic development of Castile and to prolong for so long a time the great imbalance in the Castilian social structure: the weakness of our bourgeoisie and the absence of a bourgeoise ethic among our citizens.

In reviving the long-standing inclination of the peninsular peoples toward warlike undertakings and in facilitating the prolongation of their old time activism, the American venture confirmed the already millennial triumph of the *homo hispanus,* given to impulse instead of calculation, and to the powers of the will over those of the mind. The ease with which the Spanish could root themselves on the land and live from the work of others reaffirmed in them the seignorial style of life proper to the nobility during the Middle Ages and extended it beyond the restricted ranks of the noble class as the sought-after archetype of existence. The possibility of obtaining sudden . . . riches kept open the doors that would permit one to rise in status and conserved the traditional fluidity of social classes in Castile. Those who experienced the novelty of reaching a high social rank became the zealous guardians of the traditions of the upper class into which they had entered and thus created the somber façade of *hidalguismo.*

The magnitude of the success achieved and the astonishing changes of fortune that came about prolonged the old strains of Spanish pride. The crudeness and the difficulty of the struggle in which life was gambled at every step and the hard, rough existence in the new settlements, perpetually at war with the land and the Indians, sharpened the edges of the already steely personality of the conquistadors and colonists. This, and the lack of close ties, which result from lasting residence from father to son in the same urban center—family connections, common traditions, common miseries and hopes—accentuated Spanish individualism and exalted their explosive egos.

An examination of the ways in which the American involvement—at once chimerical and adventurous—affected the psyche and the talent or functional contexture of the Spanish people could be extended to many other aspects of our way of life and could be deepened and detailed minutely. But what has been said is enough to prove that, as I said twenty-five years ago, the similarity between the two great stages of Spanish history—the medieval reconquest and repopulation of the peninsula and the later conquest and colonization of America—contributed to prolong, and in truth, perpetuate the whole complex of strengths and weaknesses of the peninsular way of life that had been erected on the foundations of the primitive heritage of northern Spain in the course of the age-old struggle between Spain and Islam.

2

CHARLES VERLINDEN

ITALIAN INFLUENCES
IN IBERIAN COLONIZATION

Although few historians would agree with Robert S. Lopez, who has suggested that the Spanish Empire under Philip II was "almost an economic colony of Genoa,"* the importance of Italians in bringing the Iberian empires into being cannot be denied. It was the Genoese who conceived the vision of far-flung commerce with the Orient, the Genoese who opened the windows onto a wider world for the parochial Iberians, and they who provided so much of the capital necessary for the voyages of exploration and discovery. In the following selection, Charles Verlinden, who has been the most assiduous cultivator as well as ardent defender of Italian influences in Iberian expansion, gives a brief but comprehensive account of the participation of Italian merchants in the late medieval Iberian economy, as well as discussing some

From Charles Verlinden, "Italian Influences in Iberian Colonization," *The Hispanic American Historical Review,* XXXIII (1953), 199–211. Reprinted by permission of the author and *The Hispanic American Historical Review.*
* Robert S. Lopez, "Market Expansion, the Case of Genoa," *The Journal of Economic History,* XXIV (1964), 461–462.

of the problems connected with the subject that still remain to be explored.

Born in 1907, Charles Verlinden was a pupil of the great Belgian medievalist, Henri Pirenne, at the University of Ghent, where he now holds a Professorship in European History in addition to being Director of the Belgian Institute in Rome. Although Professor Verlinden's early work was primarily concerned with the Crusades, throughout his career he has maintained a special interest in the history of the Iberian peninsula. Along with his work on the Latin Empire of Constantinople, he has published a price history of the Low Countries, as well as the first volume of his monumental study of slavery in medieval Europe: L'Esclavage dans l'Europe médiévale, Péninsule Ibérique-France.

When studying the beginnings of modern colonization, one must always remember that the Spaniards and Portuguese, who occupied the stage almost alone for more than a century, had the opportunity to make use of the experience gathered by the Italians and above all by the Genoese in the technique of commerce in general, as well as especially in the field of colonial economy, as this economy had gradually developed in their possessions in the Levant and on the shores of the Black Sea. Many features, characteristic of the economic and colonial activity of the Iberian nations, can only be understood when their connection and resemblance with Italian precedents is kept in mind.

Italy was the only really colonizing nation during the middle ages. From the beginning of the crusades onwards, Venice, Pisa, Genoa, later Florence, and southern Italy under the Angevins as well as under the Aragonese, were interested in the Levant and in the economic and colonial possibilities offered there by the gradual waning of the Byzantine empire. It is also at about the same time that

Italian merchants appear in the Iberian peninsula, and obtain an influence that will persist until far into the modern period, both in European and colonial economy.

Some facts, for instance the presence of a large number of Italians in Seville and Lisbon in the times of Henry the Navigator, Columbus and Vasco da Gama, are well known. But how and when did those Italians arrive there? What kind of influence did they exert? . . .

Pisans and Genoese appear in Catalonia at the beginning of the twelfth century. They draw Spain and Portugal into the sphere of the "international" trade of the time. Everywhere along the shores of the Iberian peninsula they create centers for an activity marked by long-distance maritime trade. They seem the torch-bearers of economic progress and surround the peninsula as a wood-shed to which they set fire from every side. But destruction is not brought by them; new life awakes which they help to keep active together with Iberian merchants and seamen.

Everywhere, thus, along the eastern and western coasts of the Iberian peninsula Italians animate during the twelfth century the economic revival and the long-distance sea trade. Genoese and Pisans play the leading part. During the thirteenth century the influence of the Genoese increases, that of the Pisans falls behind.

In Castile the importance of the Genoese continually increases from the middle of the century onwards. When Seville is taken by the Christians, in 1248, Genoa immediately is granted far-reaching privileges. In 1251, King Ferdinand III bestows on it a whole quarter with *fondaco*, chapel, oven, and bath. The taxation of the Genoese is fixed, and the relations of their consuls with the Castilian authorities are regulated. The oil trade, to which many of them give their time and money, leads to their permanent presence in Seville and makes them ask for citizenship in order to become *vecinos* of the town. The charter of 1251 that regulates their status is the starting-point for their subsequent legal condition during the whole of the later middle ages.

This Genoese *barrio* in Seville during the thirteenth and fourteenth centuries is the foremost center of activity in the Iberian peninsula for the subjects of the Ligurian Republic. A great many Genoese tradesmen are also settled there. The Genoese are even so numerous that they are able to play a part in the conflicts in which Castile is involved and above all in the wars on the sea. It is via the colony at Seville that the first Genoese to serve Castile as an admiral, Ugo Vento, became acquainted with King Alfonso X and was appointed by him. He paved the way for a series of his countrymen such as Benedetto Zaccaria, Egidio and Ambrosio Boccanegra, and later, Christopher Columbus. . . . Already, during the thirteenth century, some Genoese are acting as money-lenders in favor of the Castilian king, but this happens more frequently from the fourteenth century onward, when some Placentines equally play a part in this financial business that had become a specialty to them. In 1310, one Giovanni de Vivaldo, whose kinship with the celebrated traveler of the same name should be investigated, lends sums to the king of Castile. The same occurs with a member of the illustrious family of the Spinola. Some of these businessmen collect municipal taxes. Thus, in 1381, one Gaspar Cibon (Ital. Cibo) *"genoes"* is busy as *"canbiador e recabdador del dinero de la carne."* Already, in 1370, a prominent Genoese known as Micer Gaspar and no doubt identical with our Cibo, lends funds on several occasions to the town council. The fact that these Genoese of the fourteenth century are busy in Seville in public and private finance, prepares their successors for the task of money-lenders they fulfill in the time of the great discoveries, and enables them to act their parts in the Castilian civil service, a role they will be reluctant to give up for centuries.

In Portugal Italian influence during the thirteenth century is scarcely known. But it is certain that Italians dealt with several aspects of economic life such as the whale and coral fishery in Algarve and especially in Lagos. They become principally numerous after that, at the end of the thirteenth and the beginning of the fourteenth century when Italian convoy navigation to northwestern Europe is growing important. From this period onward the coasts of Spain and Portugal are navigated by Genoese, Venetian, and later on also by Florentine and sometimes Neapolitan convoys bound to England and Flanders. In this way Lagos became, from about 1310, an important harbor on the route of the Italian convoys to northwestern Europe. If one remembers that Lagos, much more than Sagres, was the starting point of the first Portuguese discoveries, the importance of the bonds, established there with Italian seamen and businessmen, grows evident.

This Italian convoy navigation was, during the whole of the fourteenth and fifteenth centuries, of the foremost significance for Spain and Portugal. To prove this, it will be sufficient to quote, for instance, the regulation of the Florentine Consuls of the Sea of 1447 that fixed the list of the ports where the galleys bound to Flanders had to anchor. In Spain and Portugal these ports were San Feliú de Guixols in Catalonia, Palma in Mallorca, Valencia, and then still more to the South, Javea, Villajoyosa, Denia, Alicante, Almería, Málaga and, beyond the Strait of Gibraltar, Cádiz, Lisbon and La Coruña. The other Italian convoys entered these or other Iberian ports. All of them had an influence on the organization of Spanish and Portuguese convoys to the colonies in the Atlantic and the Indian Ocean that has been nearly completely neglected until now. When it becomes possible to do so systematically, it will be worth while to compare carefully the late medieval Italian with the early modern Spanish and Portuguese practice of convoy navigation; the more since we know that in both Iberian countries Italians played a leading part in the organization of this kind of transportation.

Actually Italian influence in Iberian colonization starts with the period during which Italian convoy navigation was growing really important, i.e., the fourteenth century. This may, at first sight, look somewhat paradoxical, since it is generally assumed that in Portugal the period of the great discoveries begins with Henry the Navigator, who took the lead after the conquest of Ceuta, in 1415. As for Spain, it is even frequently stated that nothing of importance occurred before the first voyage of Columbus in 1492. I believe that further study will make it necessary to give up such assumptions and that the history of Portuguese colonization will have to start with the reign of Affonso IV (1325–1357), while for Spain, above all for Castile, colonization hardly begins later. This calls for a few words of explanation.

In 1317 King Diniz of Portugal had introduced into his country the Genoese merchant family of the Pessagno and since then a series of its members held, during nearly two centuries, the highest positions in the Portuguese navy. Such admirals were not only in command of the fleet; they also built ships and were concerned with trade and exploration. Lanzarotto Malocello, who discovered the Canary Islands between 1325 and 1339, was a Genoese acquainted with the Pessagno and had probably traded with them to England.

From this time, Portugal, Castile, and Aragon were interested in the Canary archipelago. It was made a rule to promise feudal concessions to those who intended to discover and take possession of new territory. The same practice had long been a habit in Italian colonial procedure, especially among the Genoese. . . .

The expeditions to the Canary Islands went on during the whole fourteenth century, and gradually other archipelagos were explored and colonized with the same methods. With all these events, whether for Portugal or for Castile, Italians were always concerned. Till now we knew this principally for a later time. Pedro Fernández Cabrón, for instance, with whom a contract is concluded by Ferdinand and Isabella in 1480 with a view to the occupation and cultivation of some of the Canary Islands, is, in spite of his Spanish name, a true Genoese. Other Italians settled

as captains-*donatários*[1] on more than one of the Portuguese islands of the Atlantic. The most celebrated among
them is Perestrello, the father-in-law of Columbus, who
was born in Piacenza and settled in Porto Santo, one of the
Madeira Islands. But there are Italians to be found as far
as the Gulf of Guinea. . . .

Notwithstanding general belief, Portuguese colonization
was not from the very beginning a royal monopoly. For
the time of Henry the Navigator, Mrs. H. Fitzler maintains
that a large number of colonial undertakings were organized as companies. These companies were preceded by
commercial and industrial concerns in the mother country
in which Italians played a leading part. In 1456 the king
founded a company for growing and selling cork, of which
the Genoese Domenico Scotto and Marco Lomelini were
members, as well as the Florentine Giovanni Guidotti.
Nearly at the same moment that these *societates* animated
the internal economy of Portugal, colonial companies
appear with a *mesa* or board of directors, a general
assembly and a specialized management, i.e., with more
than one aspect of the colonial companies established later
on in northwestern Europe. There is a great deal of still
unexplored evidence about these questions in Portuguese
archives. But it is already apparent that the Genoese
mahone[2] have, to some extent, been the pattern for the
Portuguese achievements.

How can the role of the Italians at the beginning of
Iberian colonization be explained?

First, and above all, by the place they were able to
conquer in the key positions of the Iberian peninsula itself.
In Portugal they were as numerous in Lisbon as in Al-

---

[1] Portuguese officials charged with the settlement and administration of colonial areas entrusted to them, under various conditions, by the King. (Ed.)

[2] Companies organized for trade in the medieval Mediterranean.
(Ed.)

garve, whence the expeditions started. . . . When, in 1415, the Portuguese began their new and final expansion under Henry the Navigator with the taking of Ceuta, Italians, and first of all Genoese, were everywhere concerned with it. In several instances, the latter were in Northern Africa even before the Portuguese. And how could it have been otherwise for they had visited the markets of Morocco since the end of the twelfth century. Here, too, there exists continuity that has escaped us till now and which we should integrate into the history of Portuguese discovery and colonization.

It is not unimportant to emphasize Genoese connections with Morocco. When the Portuguese conquered Ceuta in 1415, they found there a Genoese *fondaco*. In Algiers, in 1437, in Fez in the following year, they met Genoese moneychangers. In Sale lived Genoese and Venetians, among whom several had business connections with northwestern Europe. Some were serving native kings, as did one Franco Doria, military engineer with the king of Fez. Italians were active, too, in the mountain villages of the Atlas. There they bought leather and wax and sent these wares generally to Portugal but sometimes directly to Genoa. The same occurs in Southern Morocco, although the country was a great deal more savage and colonial. Sometimes the Genoese sold weapons to the Moroccans of the time who were making the life of Portuguese garrisons difficult.

This Italian trade with Morocco had its European bases in Lisbon or Lagos as well as in Cádiz and Jerez. Thence the Italians had their part in Iberian discovery and colonization along the African coast, on the continent as well as in the archipelagoes. This was the way the Venetian, Cà da Mosto, followed to become one of the most important collaborators of Henry the Navigator during the last years of his career. And in the same manner all Italian businessmen who went to the Canary Islands, the Azores, or Madeira established connections with the Portuguese or Castilian courts.

.   .   .

From the beginning of the fifteenth century representatives of the Genoese nobility settled in Jerez. They came there—just as they had to Seville at the end of the thirteenth century—with their ships, which they hired out to the king of Castile, but used also for trade, when no military duties engaged them. We know these men from the deeds of a Jerez notary called Hernando de Carmona . . .

The Spinola and the di Negro[3] played a primary part here. As the latter were intimately acquainted with the Banco di S. Giorgio[4]—which in Genoa was concerned with the Levant possessions and for a time directed them—one can be aware immediately of the influence they might have exerted on the first development of Spanish colonial administration and especially on the Casa de Contratación.

The Genoese of Cádiz, Jerez, Puerto Santa María, and San Lúcar de Barrameda were very busy with trade with the Portuguese *presidios* in Africa, with the Azores, Medeira and the Canary archipelago. Numerous among them were the factors of the di Negro, Centurioni, Cibo, Franchi, and other great families. They moved frequently, as did many businessmen and firms later on to play their part in the trade with America, to conquer their position in the Iberian colonial economy by first maintaining relations with the oldest colonial zone, which already during the fifteenth century was in full expansion on the shores and archipelagoes of northwestern Africa.

Many among the Genoese of Jerez and Cádiz went there when and because the Turks went forward in the Levant. As the Genoese colonies in the eastern part of the Mediterranean were waning, they became interested still more in the growing Iberian *imperium* in Africa. They hoped to have part in the earnings by settling in Portuguese and Spanish districts in which trade with the colonies developed. At the same time they had at their disposal good

---

[3] Important merchant families of Genoa. (Ed.)
[4] The state bank of the city of Genoa. (Ed.)

relay-stations along the convoy lines to northwestern Europe. From Seville and the southern Iberian ports they will, later on, easily trade with America. It looks as though Genoese colonization, after the loss of the Levant, was going on in the West, but now under foreign sovereignty.

As to the African archipelagoes, this activity persisted even when relations with America had already started. . . . The Genoese, Lorenzo Cattaneo, for instance, buys on one occasion in 1500, 50.000 *arrobas* of sugar in Madeira, while the Florentines Marchione and Sernigi also play an important part in this trade.

Besides, sugar cane, according to Duarte Pacheco Pereira in his *Esmeraldo de situ orbis,* was introduced into Madeira from Sicily. Later on, in Brazil, sugar-growing came in via Madeira, thanks to both the Genoese Adorno and the Antwerp merchant Schetz. If one keeps in mind that the Adorno were also interested in sugar-growing in Sicily and that some of them were settled in Jerez and in Portugal, whence Madeira, Brazil, and all the other sugar-growing districts of the Atlantic could easily be reached, the question arises whether this is not a kind of big concern about which we should like to know more.

The part of the Genoese in the colonization of Tenerife in the Canarian archipelago has been studied very recently in an excellent paper by Señorita Manuela Marrero. Nevertheless, the evidence gathered there is only available for the years between 1496 and 1509, and more facts should be put at our disposal. This is really possible, thanks to the existence in Tenerife of well-preserved town and notarial archives.

In 1496 Alonso de Lugo, with royal Castilian consent and Italian financial participation, founded a company for the conquest and exploration of the island of La Palma. The Italian capitalists were awarded territorial concessions, among which some were operated by companies, a feature to be found also in the Levant possessions of the Italian republics.

Manpower was partly supplied by trade in black and

Guanche slaves in which Spaniards as well as Italians were very busy. Immediately, grain is raised and marshland is drained. One Italian gives land away by subinfeudation, just as it so often occurred in the Levant. Genoese play the leading part, but there are also Romans, Lombards, and Venetians. Without Italian capital and Italian experience the development of colonial economy in the archipelago would have been much slower. Still more important, the same may be said for Spanish, as well as for Portuguese, America.

As for Brazil, the company created in 1502 for trade in brazilwood, got its financial means from Portuguese and *maranos*,[5] but also from Genoese and Florentines. Among the latter was the Marchione firm we have already met on Madeira. It is probably as a factor of Marchione that Americo Vespucci undertook his first voyage in 1503.

But I should like to insist principally upon the part of the Seville Italian colony at the beginning of the trade with America. . . .

A large number of these Italians from Seville went to America and settled there. When ordinances are issued prohibiting them from remaining in the Spanish colonies they escape this difficulty by naturalization. In this way they were able to introduce into the New World their methods as well as their technique. This can be noticed especially in the exchange business, in which they had gathered vast experience. They were interested, too, in mining to such an extent that in the second half of the sixteenth century Peru counted many naturalized Genoese among its inhabitants.

In the trade with America several Florentines also play an important part. On the other hand, Venetians are nearly completely absent. The explanation is obvious. In opposition to what occurred for the other Italian colonies, those which Venice owned in the Levant remained in her possession until far into the seventeenth century. Venice was not

---

[5] Iberian Jews. (Ed.)

compelled to search in America for the advantages that Genoa and Florence were no longer able to find in the Levant. Furthermore, the political constellation of the time also had its part in these circumstances.

Whenever Italians entered into a company with Spaniards, they invested more money than the latter. Hence they succeeded in getting still more control over colonial trade. And since a great deal of the financial power of the Spanish monarchy depended on this kind of commerce, they could gradually attract state finance into their sphere of influence. Here too the Genoese were the leaders.

When studying the Genoese methods in the Spanish colonial trade, A. Sayous emphasizes that it is impossible to understand the working of Spanish companies for American commerce without knowledge of Italian medieval precedents, such as *commenda* and *societas maris*.[6] For the explanation of the contracts he uses the *Suma de tratos y contratos* by Tomaso de Mercado (Seville, 1571) but fails to remark that the sponsor of this Spanish economist, Angelo Bruengo, is also an Italian, about whom we should like to be better informed.

Although he supplies many useful data, Sayous, in general, has set in a wrong way the problem of Italian influence. There is more than one reason for this. Sayous, as has already been said, could use only the catalogue of the Seville notaries. Furthermore, he did not really insist upon concrete comparison with late medieval Italian methods, above all with those concerning the Levant colonies. Besides, he did not try to investigate in what kind of economic atmosphere Italian influence took root in Spanish soil and in the colonies. This has been impossible for him, since he neglected to examine the late medieval Spanish economy systematically.

Sayous also believed that insurance had only reached a very slight development in Seville and that the old technique of the sea loan was generally used with Italians

---

[6] On the *commenda*, see the Introduction. (Ed.)

acting as moneylenders. Where this actually occurs, the reason is not the alleged backward state of Spanish commercial law, since legislation about sea-insurance was highly developed in Spain during the sixteenth century. Even on the basis of the very incomplete information used by the French scholar, one may notice that the contents of the company contracts concluded for American trade are much more extensive and complicated than the generally very short Italian *commenda* or *societas maris* agreements of the thirteenth century. This is an evident consequence of the fact that Italian commercial practice went on developing during the later middle ages, and that the Spanish economic atmosphere also exerted its influence.

. . . I hope to have made evident that Italian influence was really very important in Iberian colonization during the later middle ages and early modern times. I hope to have emphasized, too, that this influence deserves an extensive systematic treatment, but, for such an investigation, it should always be kept in mind that external influence combines with internal development. There exists no Italian nor Spanish, nor Portuguese history of such evolution; there is only the general western one.

TWO

❄

ELEMENTS OF
CONQUEST AND
SETTLEMENT

VIRGÍNIA RAU

THE MADEIRAN SUGAR CANE PLANTATIONS

With the occupation and settlement of the Atlantic islands, a new chapter in the saga of sugar began. Either uninhabited (Madeira) or sparsely populated (the Canary Islands), these islands offered ideal conditions, socially and climatically, for the growing of sugar cane. In the next selection Virgínia Rau describes the peculiar characteristics of production on the island of Madeira and indicates the extent to which this experience may be seen as a "trial run" for the sugar-based economy of sixteenth-century Brazil. Her description of the separation between production, which was largely in Portuguese hands, and marketing, which was controlled by Genoese merchants, is of particular significance, since this formed a basic pattern that continued into Portugal's Atlantic economy in the next century.

Virgínia Rau, until recently Dean of the Faculty of Letters at the University of Lisbon, took both her licentiate and her doctorate at that institution. She

From Virgínia Rau, "The Settlement of Madeira and the Sugar Cane Plantations," *Afdelung Agrarische Geschiedinis Bijdragen,* XI (1964), 3–12. Reprinted by permission of the author.

remained there to teach and, before becoming Dean, was Professor of Portuguese History and head of the Center of Historical Studies at the university. During the last two decades she has written many important works, ranging from studies of Portuguese prehistory to problems of Brazilian trade in the eighteenth century. The selection presented here represents part of her continuing interest in and study of the island of Madeira.

The study of the colonization of Madeira is of outstanding interest for its characteristics. In the first place, it was the colonization of an uninhabited island where no cattle or food plants existed. In the second place—besides its great inherent economic importance—because Madeira was also used as a "test field"—an experimental station, as Vítor Viana called it—where methods and techniques were tried out which were afterwards applied on a larger scale in the other Atlantic islands and later in Brazil and Africa. The island of São Tomé was the crucial point of transition where the sugar cane began to be grown in a tropical climate. At a very early stage, traces could be found there of the "advance" of sugar cultivation which, starting from Madeira and throughout the last twenty-five years of the fifteenth century, ended by attaining the shores of the Brazilian northeast in the first quarter of the sixteenth century. The production of São Tomé island was sufficiently important in 1517 to warrant the drawing up of "sugar sale regulations."

But the relationship with Brazil—a relationship so close that a great many Madeirans have already been traced in Brazilian colonization in the sixteenth and seventeenth century—offers a suitable field for study, though it should not make us forget the special characteristics of the colonization of Madeira. The technical conditions of sugar production and the juridical conditions of land tenure and exploitation typical of an island isolated in the Atlantic reveal entirely distinct and new economic aspects in a likewise different politico-administrative framework.

The differences relating to Brazil, are generally speaking, very relevant, well known and, we may say, indisputable. From another point of view, the colonization of Madeira is the first undertaking of modern colonization. It was carried out under exceptional conditions owing to the nonexistence of a prior population and of a prior local production structure, even of a primitive type, and Christian Europe had never undertaken anything of the kind till then. When manpower, sundry techniques and juridical and political structures were transplanted to Madeira Island, there were no native obstacles or different work techniques to surmount. But there was indeed the adaptation of a technical equipment and of a juridico-social structure suited to the climate and production conditions of the Continent to a wholly new area which, though fertile, was wild, that is to say, had not been previously prepared. This fact entailed great alterations and adjustments and required a selection of adaptable productive crops (besides subsistence crops: cereal crops and others). Of all these, the one that would yield more immediate results was sugar cane. We should not forget that as early as 1404, at least, sugar cane was being grown in the Algarve (Southern Portugal) and in 1451 in the Coimbra area. Very early references (1433) to this crop in Madeira with a view to exportation are extant. At the end of the fifteenth century the volume of its production was already internationally felt: "It is produced today [1493] in such volume that the whole of Europe has more sugar than is customary," wrote Nuremberg travelers. Historians have considered this fifteenth century event as a "remarkable success": the sugar trade "was the most important among the trade of all other products from the two archipelagos of Madeira and the Azores." Indeed, this international boom was soon recorded in European markets as being in the ascendant (a fact which was already apparent in Bristol in 1466 and in Flanders in 1468), and the production of 400 "*cântaros*" (pitchers) reported by Cadamosto in 1455 was mostly intended for external consumption. Thus occurred a truly extraordinary phenomenon, viz., an entirely uninhabited wooded island being placed under cultivation and changed in the space of thirty years into a considerably important producing center for exportation, in regular connection with a continent which some time before had no knowledge of its existence. We have here a striking instance of the creative capacity of adaptation of man, who based on prior experience, renews such experience and adapts it intelligently to previously unforeseen circumstances.

Some historians saw in the colonization of Madeira a typically medieval product. We are not going to discuss this point of view here as a thesis; we shall restrict ourselves to contributing some data which we think may be useful for its analysis.

Knowledge of the existence of Madeira in the Middle Ages has been much discussed. In these discussions, often tainted by priority considerations, it is forgotten that the essential fact in this case is the exploitation of an island with very promising conditions, an exploitation undoubtedly connected with the technical control of navigation in the Atlantic. Up to the fifteenth century, Madeira, whether known or not, could not be peopled; no one knew how to get there and come back at will—a fundamental operation achieved by the fifteenth century Portuguese, who thus gave human existence to these Atlantic islands.

. There is not many available quantitative data on Madeira sugar, nor on area under cultivation, number of mills in existence, or even general production. We shall thus have to reproduce here the scanty known figures and the estimates made from them. In fact, what we have are Cadamosto's references (although subject to certain equivalences owing to the unit of measurement he adopted, the "*cântaro*," or pitcher), the license of construction of Diogo de Teive's mill in 1452, and the letters of acquittance of the last quarter of the fifteenth century. These widely spaced references render difficult an analysis of the development of sugar cane in Madeira, since the available data to determine this process are of a predominantly juridical nature, much less amenable to the factors acting on immediate economic dynamics. Yet, even from this point of view, the case of Madeira was typical and pointed to the future. Madeira being an island in the middle of the Atlantic, and producing an established item of export of guaranteed consumption, production estimates soon assumed there an eminently practical interest, as they were connected with substantial private economic interests (both national and foreign). The fate of sugar "regards the profit and welfare not only of the said island but also of our entire kingdom." Hence the estimates or production calculations made to facilitate the solution of fiscal, evaluation, collection and contract-granting problems, or to ascertain the possibilities of selling and placing this crop in the various international markets open to Madeira sugar, which had to compete with sugar from Sicily, Egypt and the Canary Islands. The "Book of the Superintendent of the Royal Domains for Funchal Sugar," year 1494, contains a detailed estimate of sugar production in that year, viz., 80,451 "arrobas" (1 arroba = 15 kgs.). This estimate, made by the official assessors, is the oldest known for that "colonial" produce and was carried out when the island was in full development. It preceded the appearance of the diseases that began to attack the sugar cane, perhaps after 1502, and also the decree of August 21, 1498, whereby the exportation of Madeira sugar was limited to 120,000 "arrobas," and brings before us the production of the island in what may be described as a boom period.

What we know about sugar cane growing in Madeira has extremely interesting aspects. It is possible that the frequent references to the great plantation of the Esmeraldos have misled us till today in two respects which we shall now analyze. In the first place, the data contained in the estimation of 1494 show us a sugar-cane cultivation organized in a regime of medium and small plantations, even when these expressions are applied to Madeira. By this we mean rural landowners having a production of 1,500 "arrobas," which would be inadequate for the "great" Brazilian or Portuguese estates.

It should be stressed that in the Southern districts land tenure was much more broken up and of smaller size. The overwhelming majority was constituted by low and middle bracket landowners whose production only exceeded 250 "arrobas" under very exceptional conditions. As may be seen, it is impossible to speak here of "large estates," which in some areas may be even considered as nonexistent. But the perspective is confirmed and corrected as to accuracy from another point of view more directly connected with the process of exploitation when we look into the figures of the assessments made.

The estimates, of course, regarded "cultivation units" which were not necessarily identical. It is found, however, that the cultivation unit came to practically half the figure given for the producing average per grower. If the estate was not large, the exploitation unit was even smaller. This conclusion is further stressed in the classification of the production of such units as reported to the assessors.

It will thus be seen that we are still far from the great sugar-cane plantations of future Brazil, with their slavery institutions and their great mill and plantation owners. What predominated in Madeira was a landed middle class with limited possibilities which, in any case, were seldom sufficient to enable its members to keep up a system of production based on slavery—an expensive system when used in connection with small units. We do not mean by this, of course, that no slaves were employed in the island's sugar-cane plantations; our intention is only to explain the restricted character of slavery there.

The average cultivation area under each landowner or producer was not, in fact, very great. It is perhaps necessary to analyze at this point the share of each rural landowner or producer in production as a whole.

We find that in the "cool" lands of the Southwest of the island one-fifth of the landowners had under their charge half of the production of that area. At Funchal, in the older central part of the Southern area of sugar-cane growing, land property was entirely medium and low bracket.

And if we turn once again from the plantation to production units, the concentration increases, though the production units appear to be of medium or comparatively small size. There is here an aspect of great social significance, and also in the existence of a great number of small producers. Every single one of the ten greatest plantation owners at Funchal had a share in local production ranging between 6.5 percent and 2.3 percent.

To offset this, about two thirds of plantation owners had a participation under 1 percent, over half of them having 0.5 percent as their share. This is a very curious phenomenon which places us before a markedly characteristic social reality: sugar production spelled profit to wide strata of the population and among sugar producers—besides low- and middle-bracket farmers—there were shoemakers, carpenters, barbers, merchants, surgeons, millers. These peoples were rubbing shoulders with noblemen, municipal officials and others who picked the crumbs of the benefits accruing from this wealth-bringing crop—a very different reality from the one usually suggested when the social panorama of the island of Madeira in the sixteenth century is depicted. All this motley crowd of small producers availed themselves of a distribution organization set up in the island to render their minute production profitable.

The second aspect to be stressed is the national or Portuguese character of sugar production. Frequent mention is made of the intervention of Flemish, Italian and Catalan farmers in the production of Madeira sugar. But in this estimate the foreign sugar-producing element in Funchal is of very restricted economic significance.

It is found that about seventy years after the beginning of the colonization of Madeira the participation of foreigners in sugar production, even after such production was firmly established in European markets, remained very small. It should not be concluded from this, however, that foreigners had little to do with the sugar trade.

In this way, it is possible to distinguish and place against its proper background the problem or—more impressively —the tragedy of islands in general and of Madeira in particular whenever their situation as islands—therefore an isolated situation—is rendered worse by a production regime. Not one of monoculture, as thought by Fernand Braudel, but where the economy of the island is tied to the income from a given product. Here we unearth the roots of an important point to stress, which is the disjointing between the direct production regime entrusted to nationals in its overwhelming majority and the system of distribution and marketing, mostly left to foreigners. The soil-bound producer, having no means of placing his crop (and therefore almost unable to augment by himself the value of the product), was subject to the price and conditions imposed by the merchant, who controlled the distribution machinery and had access to European markets. In this case—and in how many others?—the merchant was often a foreigner acquainted with the markets of Flanders, Italy, England, etc., and who had his own circle of clients and his own capital; the producer was a Portuguese with his own land, his own property, his own religion and his own language. Clashes were unavoidable and often occurred. Thus we have the statements of the alderman Mem Rodrigues at a meeting of the Town Council of Funchal on July 18, 1472, to the effect that the trade of sugar and all the rents of the islands, were placed in the hands of certain men whose superintendent was a Genoese, Messer Leão, and that it would be advisable to transfer the factory to Portuguese hands because in a number of localities some "places" had been destroyed, damaged and lost owing to the presence of Genoese. Complaints were made at the Cortes of 1472–1473 that the sugar trade was in the hands of Genoese and Jews, it being requested that, after the lapse of the contract of the island of Madeira, the purchase and sale of the said sugar should be open to all. There were complaints also in 1481–1482 against the fact that Madeira sugar was not sent to Lisbon for redistribution. The prohibition of residence to foreigners was demanded as well as the expulsion of foreigners from the island and the cancellation of residence permits. The monopolist projects of Duke Dom Fernando (1469) and later of King John II were criticized; and the fixation of the exportable quotas and the ascribing of certain amounts to each market were asked for. The aim of all this was to curtail foreign intervention or to ensure direct participation in the profits from the external market. Obviously these efforts were of no avail or redundant. The foreigners had control of the markets and sometimes of the material means of access to them: the economic "respiration" of the island was to a large extent in their power. This fact is of undoubted importance to understand Duke Dom Fernando's plan, conceived in 1469, of establishing a sugar monopoly; a plan which the Madeirans resisted by applying for its revocation, which they succeeded in bringing about. Viewing the problem from a distance, it becomes apparent that a monopoly was, in fact, the only means (albeit a very expensive one) of counteracting the external influence of merchants or foreigners. The Duke, if he had the whole production under his control, would be in a position to set up his own system of distribution, in which the merchants would naturally share so as to "ensure some measure of remedy and correction" of the low price of sugar and to avoid any dangerous reaction in Bruges from the wealthy merchants of Sicilian sugar. On the other hand, it might bring about an even heavier economic oppression. Of two evils, the sugar producers chose the lesser one: the system of competition among foreigners, who flocked to the island or settled there attracted by the profits derived from an expensive product.

Madeira sugar was thus situated within the range of action of a "company" of certain known Portuguese and Italian traders: Martim Anes Boa Viagem, Alvaro Esteves, Fernão Pires, Baptista Lomellini, Francisco Calvo, Vicente Gil, Fernão Nunes Boa Viagem, Pedro Botelho and Messer Leão. We suspect, however, that Genoese interests were predominant in this group of traders—a supposition partly based on the fact that Baptista Lomellini obtained on November 27, 1471, that he, his factors and his company should be held as "natives of these parts," and that on December 30, 1476, the Infanta Dona Beatriz recommended him to the Funchal Town Council not as a foreigner but as a "native and her own servant."

Thus began the tragedy of the Madeirans who, after having sacrificed their subsistence crops to sugar cane growing, felt the need of "bread." In addition, sugar was beginning to cross the boundary-line of heavy production and to effect the adjustment of the critical problems connected with it—over-production and a drop in prices. In 1469, the cost of an "arroba" ranged, depending on quality, between 650 and 800 "reais," while in 1496 it ranged already between 350 and 600 "reais" in the same conditions. At the same time, there began the wave of "regulations" fixing production in accordance with the already referred to exportable totals and market quotas.

From the foregoing data it appears to us, therefore, that we shall only be able to understand the problems of the economic history of Madeira if we bear in mind the duality of national producers and predominantly foreign exporters.

We are thus led to suppose that the Genoese and Florentines were the great intermediaries in the exportation and sale of Madeira sugar after the middle of the fifteenth century. Indeed, it was then that the trade policy of some Italian republics began to look indisguisedly towards the south and Atlantic regions of Western Europe. On the one hand, there was a noticeably growing increase of Genoese commercial influence in the kingdom of Granada, and on the other hand, in general terms, of Italian predominance

in the Castilian and Portuguese world. Hence the antago-
nism between Portuguese and Italians so often brought to
expression at the Cortes. At the Lisbon Cortes of 1459, the
representatives of the people applied for the expulsion of
the Genoese and Florentines from the kingdom alleging
that they harmed the country without bringing any profit
to it. At the Coimbra-Evora Cortes of 1472–1473 and at
the Evora Cortes of 1481–1482, the protests of the
"people" were centered on their predominance in the
Madeira sugar trade, and no hesitation was felt in stating
that the Florentines and Genoese had never done anything
in Portugal except extracting gold and silver coinage from
the country and laying bare the king's secrets relating to El
Mina and the islands.

Exactly when Genoa was losing interest in her Oriental
positions and transferring her activities to the Atlantic
West, Madeira sugar began to weigh strongly in Western
production and to make possible the change of a luxury
product into a "great commodity" whose use as food was
generalized. Integrated as the island of Madeira was in the
Portuguese market, where the Genoese and Florentines
had fought their way to a dominant position, the latter at
once devoted themselves to this profitable trade, opening to
Madeira sugar an ever greater and ampler market both in
the North of Europe and in the Mediterranean. After the
second half of the fifteenth century, and more particularly
during its last quarter, Italian merchants were among the
main "exploiters" of the sugar island, and we often stumble
upon their names. João António Cesare, a Genoese, was
endeavoring to establish himself in Madeira around 1480.
Paulo di Negro, residing in Lisbon, accepted an order from
Luis Centurione, a Genoese patrician, for 2,000 "arrobas"
of sugar, and in 1478 entrusted that commercial operation
in Madeira to Christopher Columbus. In the last quarter of
the fifteenth century, Luis Doria, Urbano and Baptista
Lomellini had already taken up residence at Santa Cruz,
Santana and Porto do Seixo in the island of Madeira.
Antonio Spinola, whose beginnings had been in the wheat

trade around 1472, was already a resident of the island when he obtained his naturalization papers on May 28, 1490. In 1498 Dom Manuel, when according shipping preference to Portuguese exporters of Madeira sugar, granted to the Florentines Bartolomeo Marchionni and Jerónimo Sernigi the privilege of being included among "the native merchants." In 1500, the Genoese Lourenço Cattaneo made a contract with the king of Portugal whereby the latter sold him 50,000 "arrobas" of Madeira sugar at the rate of 400 "reais" per "arroba." In 1503, Lázaro Merello and his son Giobatta founded a commercial company with the brothers Domingos, Bernardo and Pantaleão de Sampierdarena to trade in Madeira sugar and "camellotto" between Genoa, Vicenza and Mantua.

And since the Italians succeeded in penetrating the export trade of Madeira sugar assisted by a far-flung commercial and financial network which spread all over Europe, it was no less easy for them, too, to penetrate in time the sector of land ownership, thus becoming producers and landowners in the island of Madeira. If fifteenth century Spain was a country were Genoese bankers reigned and thrived, Madeira was probably for the Italians, to a great extent, an island where an intense trade in sugar exportation was carried on throughout the second half of the fifteenth and the first half of the sixteenth century, until the advent and triumph of the great sugar export trade of Brazil in the middle of the latter century.

We referred above to heavy production on a fifteenth-century scale. Can these estimates, based on productivity as it was at the period when they were made, give us some data on the area under cultivation? We shall not go deeply into this calculation (which, in any case, would be difficult owing to the differences in farming methods, available labor, irrigation, etc.), but we are once again still very far from the true heavy production of Brazilian sugar in the middle of the seventeenth century. However, the social repercussions of Madeira production are proportionately great, as proved by the distribution of the income therefrom and of the production itself.

The "discoveries" and colonization were dovetailed in everyday life, not only through the importation of Madeira sugar, gold, slaves and the timber used in the building of the "tall houses" to which Zurara refers, but also from a very early date through the appearance of rents and pensions arising directly from overseas activity.

Besides these aspects of production and its direct or indirect distribution, and the revenue from Madeira sugar to which we have already referred, their "industrial" implications are equally interesting. In the first place, mention is made of some 16 sugar mills, half the figure given by Gaspar Frutuoso in "Saudades da Terra" for the end of the sixteenth century. Lippmann's figure for the beginning of the sixteenth century—150 mills—seems, to be quite frank, an exaggeration.

Besides the absence of foreigners and the various social strata from which mill owners came, the disparity in the volumes of production is to be stressed and indicates, no doubt, that these mills did not exist only for own production. Also in this case we cannot find any counterparts of the great "industrial" units which were to become so frequent in the Brazilian scene of the seventeenth and eighteenth centuries. We are, too, still very far from the swarms of slaves which it entailed. As happened with the agricultural production of the sugar cane, carried on in a regime of small or medium exploitation, we find here mills whose owners had sometimes a production under the general average ascertained for individual sugar cane plantation owners.

The other industrial activity to which reference is made in this document is fruit preserves. Preserves are mentioned in general in conjunction with lemons, citrons, oranges, pumpkins, pears and apricots. The data referred do serve only to link sugar with the other agricultural activities of the island but do not give us an exact idea concerning them. The fruit preserve sector was of an essentially private nature.

Being a rural industry linked with sugar production, its purposes included, no doubt, that of taking avail of the position of the island to provide supplies to shipping in transit. At the same time, it increased the production resources of the island and constituted a means of generally improving its economy at a time when many types of fruit could only be exported dried or preserved in sugar; it could also be used to regulate the sugar production of Madeira and keep it at market level as a defense against mercantile speculation, which naturally strove to deprive such production of any other options besides the ones accorded it by the merchants themselves.

So we find in Madeira the picture of intense and many-sided rural, industrial and commercial life, whether in its economic forms (which had more than one aspect) or in its social implications. These and these only were the aspects we wished to refer to here and which, in our opinion, it would be of special interest to stress. It would still be necessary to study questions of land tenure regime and co-exploitation of the land to which reference is made in it, as well as the place names and the entire minor history of families and men, of no small importance for the knowledge of the process of inclusion of these islands in "greater history."

A long series of great navigators passed through Madeira and left there an indelible imprint of human endeavor which could well be the mainspring of their thirst for adventure.

But besides these seamen there were also proud noblemen and humble officials and workers for whom sugar-cane growing was a wealthy source of income or just a standby supplementary to their rural and domestic economy.

4

RUTH PIKE

SLAVERY IN SEVILLE
AT THE TIME OF COLUMBUS

*Traditionally the revival, on a large scale, of planta-
tion slavery, especially in Brazil and the Caribbean,
has been considered one of the most remarkable
aspects of colonial Latin American society. Yet, as
Ruth Pike shows in the following selection, slavery
was far from unknown in the environment from
which Columbus and most of the other explorers
came; it had, in fact, been an important aspect of life
in the Mediterranean region throughout most of the
medieval period. Thus the ease and rapidity with
which it spread to America after discovery should be
no cause for surprise.*

*Ruth Pike took her B.S., M.A., and Ph.D. degrees
at Columbia University and, after short periods of
teaching at Brooklyn College and Rutgers University,
joined the faculty at Hunter College, where she is now
Associate Professor of History. Her special interest is
in the economy and society of Seville and its connec-*

From Ruth Pike, "Sevillian Society in the Sixteenth Century:
Slaves and Freedmen," *The Hispanic American Historical Review,* XLVII (1967), 344–359. Reprinted by permission of the
author and *The Hispanic American Historical Review.*

tions with Italy at the time of the great discoveries. Aside from the selection reprinted here, Professor Pike has written various articles on Seville at the beginning of the sixteenth century as well as The Genoese in Seville and the Opening of the New World.

In the sixteenth century Negro, Morrish, and Morisco slaves made up a sizable and conspicuous part of the population of Seville, a town that became, as a result of the opening of the New World, the most famous and important city in Spain. Throughout the century slaves abounded among the crowds that filled the streets of that teeming metropolis, "new Babylonia" as it was called by the literary figures of the period. They could be found in all the focal points of the city—along the wharves, in the *Arenal* (a promenade along the riverside where Sevillians liked to meet), and in the public squares and marketplaces. To many contemporaries the presence in Seville of so many slaves did much to create the cosmopolitan atmosphere for which the city was well known. Some observers went so far as to claim that there were almost as many Negro and Moorish slaves as free citizens; others compared the city to a giant chessboard containing an equal number of white and black chessmen.

While contemporary writers often exaggerated the size of the unfree population of Seville, there is no doubt that in the sixteenth century it harbored the largest slave community in Spain. We can never know their exact numbers throughout the century, but we do have fairly satisfactory statistics from a census taken by church officials in 1565. In that year Seville had 6,327 slaves, out of a total population of 85,538 people, that is, one slave for every fourteen inhabitants. Although this account does not tell us what proportion of these slaves were Negroes, Moors, or Moriscos, other sources lead us to believe that

Negroes outnumbered the other two groups, especially in the second half of the century. The majority of slaves in Seville, therefore, would appear to have been Negroes.

Sixteenth-century Sevillians found nothing new or unusual about the existence of these numerous slaves in their city. Negro slavery had been a part of its life for many centuries. We do not know when the first Africans were introduced into Seville after its reconquest from the Moslems in 1248, but the chroniclers tell us that by the end of the fourteenth century many Negro slaves had been brought there by merchants engaged in the trans-Saharian trade. During this period the municipal authorities tried to ease the rigors of servile life by allowing the Negroes certain privileges, such as the right to gather together on feast days and perform their own dances and songs. Eventually it became customary for one of them to be named by city officials as *mayoral* (steward) over the rest, with authority to protect them against their masters, defend them before the courts of law, and settle their quarrels. In a similar manner the Church, although primarily interested in conversion, also tried to ameliorate the physical conditions of slavery. During the last years of the fourteenth century the Church expressed its charitable intentions by establishing the Hospital of Our Lady of the Angels in the parish of San Bernardo to serve the Negro population. A short time later the Church made a further gesture toward incorporating Negroes into the spiritual fold by creating a Negro religious confraternity to run this hospital. In subsequent years many wealthy Sevillians helped to maintain Our Lady of the Angels; a notable donor was the Duke of Medina Sidonia, who at his death in 1463 left one thousand *maravedís* for the poor of this institution.

The duke's donation to the hospital of Our Lady of the Angels came at a time when Seville had already begun to feel the effects of the opening of West Africa by the Portuguese. Greater numbers of Negro slaves were coming into the river port, as Andalusian shipowners, including members of the highest nobility, competed with the Portuguese in organizing raiding expeditions on the West African coast. It was not until 1479 that the Spaniards finally recognized the Portuguese monopoly, and even then they did so reluctantly. Throughout the second half of the fifteenth century, Negroes were brought directly into the ports of southern Spain by Spanish shippers. Others were transported overland from Lisbon by Spanish and Portuguese merchants, a practice which accounts for the presence of Negro slaves in such frontier towns as Huelva, Badajoz, and Jerez de los Caballeros. By the reign of Ferdinand and Isabella, the Negro population of Seville had grown so large that the Catholic Kings decided to place them under greater royal supervision and control. In 1475 they appointed Juan de Valladolid, a royal servant, who was known popularly as the "Negro count," *mayoral* of the Seville Negro community.

After the discovery of the New World the constant demand for a source of cheap labor to work the mines and plantations of America increased the flow of Negroes into Seville during the sixteenth century. The city soon became one of the most important slave centers in Western Europe, second only to Lisbon. In fact the first Negro slaves introduced into the New World came from Seville, and some of them had been born in that city. During the first decades of the sixteenth century, the Spanish monarchs, anxious to keep the colonies free from religious taint, insisted that the slaves sent to America be Christians—i.e., that they should have been born in Spain or have resided there long enough to be baptized. In 1510, for example, King Ferdinand gave permission to ship as many as two hundred slaves from Seville for sale to the settlers of Hispaniola or for work on the royal properties there. Eventually slaves were shipped directly from Africa to America, though they continued to come to Seville, as well. Throughout the century, merchants, sea captains, and others brought slaves to the Sevillian market located in the heart of the business district. Here slaves were bought and sold amidst the noise and bustle of street vendors hawking their wares and future conquistadors recruiting men for their New World expeditions. Apparently they were not exhibited and sold at the block as was the custom elsewhere. Instead a group of slaves and their owner would go about the streets accompanied by an auctioneer who called out to onlookers offering them for sale. According to Cervantes in *El trato de Argel,* Christian slaves were sold in this same manner in Morocco.

The range of slave prices was wide and depended on the age, sex, and physical condition of the slave. An able-bodied slave brought a high market price, the average price being slightly lower. The lowest price would be for children, because of the element of risk and the expense of rearing them to a profit-bearing age. We can estimate some approximate average prices on the basis of figures taken from the numerous deeds of purchase and sale among the Sevillian Protocols. During the first decade of the sixteenth century, the average price paid for a slave in Seville was about twenty ducats; in the second and third decades of the century prices fluctuated between thirty or forty ducats. At mid-century a prospective buyer would have to pay from eighty to ninety ducats for an adult slave and by the last quarter of the century, a hundred ducats or more. Prices of slaves rose steadily during the course of the century, for like other commodities they were caught in the great inflationary wave that overwhelmed all Spain during this period.

Though the branding of slaves was a common practice, this cruel custom was not applied to all, nor was it considered an absolute necessity. We have many examples of unbranded slaves during this period. Some people branded their slaves as a kind of insurance. John Brooks points out that the branding of Carrizales' slaves in Cervantes' *Celoso extremeño* "may be considered significant of his character and plans." Moreover, branding was specifically used as a punishment for refractory and runaway slaves. Carrizales branded his four "white slaves" but did not apply this same treatment to his two Negro slaves, perhaps because contemporary opinion held that Moorish and Morisco slaves were deceitful and potential runaways, while Negroes were trustworthy and loyal to their masters. When they did occur, brands were not uniform in shape or location. The most frequent brand consisted of an S and a line (*clavo*), standing for *esclavo*, on one cheek and the owner's initial or mark on the other. But several other kinds were also in use. In 1500, for example, we have mention of a slave branded with a fleur-de-lis on one cheek and a star on the other. In another instance, a slave bore the full name of his owner on his face.

Most of the slaves branded and sold in Seville were destined for domestic service in the city's households. Slaves were employed in the kitchen, laundry room, and stable. They served as doorkeepers, as nursemaids for children, as attendants of adults, as valets, porters, and waiters. Contemporary literature tells us that an especially desirable accomplishment of the female slave was the ability to make fruit preserves and jellies. Since scientific treatises of the day taught that water taken by itself was harmful, orange flower, quince, peach, pear, and cherry preserves were kept on hand and offered to visitors, together with iced water. The master usually took some male slaves with him on his daily activities, perhaps as an escort on foot if he was riding. Merchants like the one portrayed by Cervantes in *El coloquio de los perros* usually went to the Exchange followed by a Negro servant. Slaves also did odd jobs in connection with their master's business. Such was the case of Juan Fernández, a mulatto slave belonging to the inspector of weights and measures in the municipal meat-market. When Fernández was called upon to testify in a lawsuit involving his master in 1598, he stated that "he always accompanied his master on his daily round of business, and that on the day in question he had delivered, on his masters orders, a special luncheon to several members of the city council."

Another especially desirable quality in a slave was the ability to sing, play, and dance, as music and dancing were popular pastimes during the period. Negroes showed particular fondness and aptitude for both music and dance and were often in great demand as entertainers at private parties and public celebrations. Loaysa in Cervantes' *Celoso extremeño* noted that three of his Negro pupils, all of them slaves of wealthy aldermen, played and sang well enough to perform in any dance or tavern. Moreover, Negroes were among the most accomplished interpreters of the numerous popular dances of the day, including the two favorites, the Zarabanda and the Chacona. Several of these dances—the Guineo, Ye-Ye, and Zarambeque or Zumbé—had a distinctly African flavor and were probably introduced into Spain by Negro slaves.

In the wealthier homes of the city slaves were considered a necessity—part of the conspicuous consumption of the period that called for long entourages of servants and for coaches, costly wearing apparel, and ornate home decoration. Nevertheless, the ownership of slaves in Seville was not confined to the wealthy classes—nobility and rich merchants—but widely distributed among all levels of the population. The deeds of purchase and sale among the Sevillian Protocols clearly show that artisans of various occupations, professional people such as physicians, lawyers, apothecaries, clergymen, and even religious orders owned household slaves. Indeed almost every family of some means had two or more of them.

Treatment of domestic slaves varied, depending greatly on the character of the owner, though in general their position did not differ substantially from that of the free servants. There is even some evidence that in Spain slaves received better treatment than free servants. Many slaves were closely bound to their masters and had their full confidence. Female slaves were particularly close to their mistresses; in the plays of Lope de Vega they are usually portrayed as their confidantes and go-betweens in their love affairs. The religious life of the slave was of great concern to the owner. Much care was taken to see that slaves performed their religious duties and that children of domestic slaves were duly baptized. Godparents, sometimes prestigious ones, were provided for slave children. As members of the Christian community, slaves were buried in their parish churches and in some instances in family vaults. It was also customary to have requiem masses said for them at the expense of their former owners. On the other hand, like free servants, slaves who committed misdemeanors were often whipped. More serious offenses could bring a form of punishment known as *pringar* or *lardear*—the dropping of pork fat, melted by a large taper, or the wax of the taper itself on the naked skin. Cervantes indicates that this was the regular punishment for fugitive slaves, but it was also used on household servants as a means of exacting information from them. Another more drastic method of dealing with incorrigible slaves was to "sell them overseas," i.e., to the Spanish colonies, or to donate them to the crown to be used as galley slaves. There were even some masters who chose to free slaves who proved to be rebellious and troublesome; in other words, they turned them out to starve. Delinquent slaves seem to have been the exception, however, and individual acts of violence committed by slaves against their masters were infrequent.

Although most slaves were well behaved, the existence of a large servile population created security problems for the municipal government. The city fathers feared that the urban slaves, led by the Moriscos, might band together and seize the town, and the official uneasiness on this score found expression in a series of municipal ordinances restricting the movements of slaves. Slaves were prohibited, for example, from carrying arms except in the company of their masters or in the performance of their regular duties. The government also placed severe limitations on the number of slaves permitted to assemble at any given time in public places such as taverns, inns, and cheap restaurants. City officials expressed concern about the gangs of slaves who frequented the Sevillian taverns both day and night, and who often became intoxicated and disorderly. A tavern brawl or any disturbance involving slaves was considered especially dangerous to public order. Furthermore, many taverns served as meeting places for members of the city's underworld who were quick to take advantage of slaves. Unscrupulous tavern owners in league with criminal elements encouraged slaves to steal in order to repay debts and later resold the booty for their own profit.

Municipal legislation curtailing the actions of slaves may have served to reassure the city fathers, but these regulations like so many other municipal ordinances were difficult to enforce. Effective policing of Seville was nearly impossible, for the city, overflowing with wealth, vice, and poverty, presented the most favorable conditions for the shelter and protection of criminals. In the words of Cervantes, Seville was "the refuge of the outcast." Criminals could usually escape the law by simply moving from one district to another, or even by fleeing to the Indies. Law officials and criminals often worked together—too many police officers were like Cervantes' "constable in charge of vagabonds" who, according to Monipodio, the thieves' chieftain, "was a friend and never came to do us harm." Thieves' jargon (*germania*) was used in common speech throughout the city, and everyone went about armed for protection. Even small boys imitated their elders, carrying small swords at their sides. Faced with so many disorderly and criminal elements the city government was hard put to maintain public order.

The presence of large numbers of slaves must have exacerbated the serious problem of policing the city. The municipal authorities had the power to curb the activities of slaves when public security was involved, but they could not interfere in the relationship between masters and slaves or in any way reduce the authority of owners. Slaveholders could be as arbitrary as they pleased with their property, while slaves, on the other hand, were subordinate to their masters' will. The owner could free his slaves whenever he was inclined to do so, but he usually did this by inserting a provision in his will. Manumission by will had advantages, for the master retained the services of the slaves as long as he needed them; the prospect of freedom encouraged good conduct on the part of the slave; and the slaveholder could depart this life with a freer conscience. Sometimes wills included trust provisions directing the slaveholder's heir to free a particular slave or slaves at his own death or after a given number of years of service. That such an arrangement could lead to difficulties, can be seen in the case of Ana, a mulatto slave belonging to the Sevillian aristocrat, Juan de Pineda. When Pineda died in 1526, he willed Ana to his grandson Pedro, with the proviso that she receive her freedom after ten years of service. Two years later Pedro died suddenly. Like his grandfather, he chose not to free Ana, but to include a trust provision for her in his will. Accordingly she was required to spend eight more years of servitude with Pedro's uncle (also named Juan de Pineda). Finally in 1537 Ana received her freedom, and one year later she emigrated to America.

On the other hand, it was not always necessary for slaves to wait until the death of their owner, for they often received their freedom in return for special services, for money payments, or for both. In 1580, for example, Diego Bello, a Seville resident who had just returned home from a trip to Peru, freed his slave Tomé because of "the services that the said slave had rendered him, especially on the voyage from Peru, in addition to the payment of 100 pesos." The enfranchisement of slave children was a particularly frequent occurrence. There were even some slave owners who because of special circumstances freed the unborn children of slaves. The priest Álvaro de Castro acted in this manner in 1526 when on the eve of his departure for Cuba he freed the yet unborn child of his slave Catalina as compensation for her separation from her husband Antonio, also a slave of the priest, who had to remain in Seville.

Besides domestic slavery there existed in Seville (as well as in the rest of Andalusia) the systematic exploitation of slave labor for profit. Many Sevillians considered the ownership of slaves an excellent capital investment and a profitable source of income. Some people were totally dependent on the earnings of their slaves, for they had no other way of obtaining a living. The use of slaves to earn money for their owners added another class of laborers to the city's large unskilled working force. They were a common sight on the Seville waterfront, where they worked as stevedores. Many could be found performing menial tasks in the famous soap factories or in the public granary. Others earned a living as porters, street vendors, and bearers of sedan chairs. There is also some evidence that they served as *corchetes* (constables), a rather unpopular calling in sixteenth-century Seville.

Though the Negro slaves worked at many occupations, the city's guilds refused to admit them. On the other hand, there were no restrictions against their employment by master craftsmen in their shops. We know that Negroes, both slave and free, were employed in many Sevillian printing shops, and that other craftsmen purchased slaves for use in their establishments. Moreover the Sevillian Protocols indicate that they were used in the trade between Seville and the New World. Several interesting examples of Negro slaves employed as business agents in America emerge from these documents. As early as 1502, a Sevillian merchant, Juan de Córdoba, sent his Negro slave and two other agents to sell merchandise for him on the island of Hispaniola. Seven years later Juan de Zafra, a Negro slave, was commissioned by his master, the well-known Sevillian physician Dr. Álvarez Chanca, to sell goods in the New World. Zafra remained in America for several years, and at his death in 1515 he was still performing the duties of a commission agent for his master. Most famous of all the Negro traders in America was Pedro Franco, who was freed by his master Franco Leardo, a wealthy and prominent Genoese merchant of Seville, just a few months before he left for America. Leardo gave him three hundred ducats and sent him to Panama as his agent, most probably under the usual four-year partnership contract (*com-*

pañia). Besides Leardo several other Sevillians entrusted
him with merchandise to be sold in the New World. Unfortunately Pedro Franco was not able to live up to the terms
of his contract with Leardo, for he died within a year after
his arrival on the Isthmus. In his last will and testament he
left all of his property to his former master.

Slaves who worked at outside jobs to support themselves
and their owners usually did not reside in their masters'
homes. Although they could be found scattered throughout
the poorer sections of Seville, their traditional quarter was
the parish of San Bernardo, located outside the city walls
in a swampy region dominated by a foul-smelling stream
called the Tagarete. This was a poor parish inhabited by
working people—gardeners employed in the nearby Alcázar, employees of the municipal slaughterhouse, and bakers
who worked in the many baking establishments in the
district. It was also a high crime area and one known for
its numerous ruffians and bullies, many of whom occasionally worked at odd jobs in the slaughterhouse.

By the last quarter of the century the population of San
Bernardo had increased so greatly that Church and municipal authorities decided to divide San Bernardo and to
create a new parish, that of San Roque. The chapel of the
Hospital of Our Lady of the Angels was chosen to serve as
a temporary parish church for San Roque, and, maintained
by the Negro religious confraternity, it remained the center
of the district's religious life until the completion of the
church of San Roque in 1585. Nine years later the confraternity purchased three lots opposite the new church and
built a chapel that they occupied in the last years of the
century.

In addition to the parishes of San Bernardo and San
Roque there were several other Sevillian barrios especially
noted for their numerous Negro, Moorish, and Morisco
residents. Many Moors and Moriscos, both slaves and
freedmen, lived in Triana (the favored quarter of the
seafaring population of Seville) and in the outskirts of that
district. In 1580 sailors from the Sicilian fleet, which had

anchored in the Guadalquivir off Triana, invaded the quarter, attacking the Moriscos and carrying many of them off as galley slaves. The Sevillian authorities, angered and shocked by this incident, and fearful of its consequences for public order, ordered the immediate freeing of the Moriscos and the restoration of their property. Furthermore, they wrote a detailed account of this episode to Philip II, who eventually directed the commander of the fleet to comply with the orders of the Seville city council.

Like Triana the parish of San Ildefonso also contained a sizable population of slaves and freedmen. During the second half of the sixteenth century there were enough mulattoes there to justify the creation of a religious confraternity. The confraternity maintained its own chapel in the parish church of San Ildefonso with a private entrance through a back door that opened into a small side street, called appropriately the "Street of Mulattoes." Contemporary literature also tells us that the plaza in front of the church of Santa María la Blanca was a favorite meeting place for Sevillian Negroes. Some of them must have lived in the neighborhood, although no evidence of their residence there has survived.

Among the Negroes who assembled in the Plaza de Santa María la Blanca were many freedmen and women. Although most Sevillian Negroes were slaves, the city also contained a significant free Negro population. Enfranchisement was not a step toward economic and social betterment, however, for Negroes and mulattoes remained on the lowest rungs of the social ladder, whether slaves or freedmen. Ex-slaves continued to work in unskilled and menial jobs and to reside in the same neighborhoods as before their emancipation. A combination of discrimination and unfavorable economic conditions prevented freedmen from rising in society. The artisans feared Negro competition and jealously excluded them from the few skilled positions which the inadequate Sevillian industry afforded. Even unskilled jobs were at a premium in Seville because of the steady flow of landless peasants from the countryside into the town. The streets of Seville were soon overrun with beggars, vagabonds, and unemployed, many of whom found no other solution than to join the Sevillian underworld. Chronic unemployment and severe food shortages were the realities of life for the majority of Sevillians throughout the sixteenth century. Popular discontent and lack of bread led to several riots during the period, the most important being the uprising of the Feria district in 1521.

Competition for jobs strained relations between freedmen and the white Sevillian laborers. The whites showed their contempt for Negroes with the customary sidewalk jeer (*estornudo*). On the individual level, however, Negroes and whites mixed freely, and contacts were friendly. Miscegenation and common-law unions were frequent. Many Sevillians, including members of the clergy, maintained illicit relations with female household slaves, and in some instances recognized their illegitimate children. Among the servant class miscegenation was common practice, and mixed marriages were not unknown.

Although Negro freedmen and slaves lived on the fringe of Sevillian life socially and economically, they enjoyed full membership in the Church. True religious conversion among newly baptized Negroes was unusual, but by the second generation many had become sincere and pious Christians. The very willingness of Negroes to become Christians and to remain faithful to their new religion facilitated their popular acceptance. In addition, their incorporation into the social and ritual activities of the Church accelerated the process of their Hispanicization. Through their parish churches and their confraternities slaves and freedmen took part in all the city-wide religious celebrations of the period. The Negro and mulatto brotherhoods marched in full regalia in the many religious processions, including those of Holy Week. On one such occasion, the dress and the insignias of the Negro brotherhood were so elaborate and costly as to draw censure from the clergy. In another instance, according to the chronicler

Ortiz de Zúñiga, a member of the Negro confraternity sold himself as a slave in order to cover the high cost of his group's participation in a religious festival. Negro performers also took part in the *autos* connected with the festival of Corpus Christi. In 1590 the city government paid eight ducats to Leonor Rija, a mulatto, to appear on a float in the Corpus Christi celebration and to sing, dance, and play the guitar together with four other mulatto women and two men.

If it was difficult for freedmen to improve their status in Seville, they might seize the opportunity to emigrate to the New World. The registers of the Casa de Contratación indicate that many Negro freedmen crossed the ocean to America during the sixteenth century. Most of these emigrants were single men and women, but we can also find instances of women with young children and of family groups. A good example was the Bonilla family—husband, wife, and two children—who signed up at the Casa de Contratación in 1515. Many freedmen accompanied their former masters to the New World as servants. In 1538, for instance, the freedman Bernardo declared that he was traveling to Florida as a valet of his ex-master Captain Pedro Calderón. A year later another freedman by the name of Domingo went to Peru with his former owner the adventurer Lope de Aguirre, whose later exploits in the Amazon region won him the unfortunate epithet of "the tyrant." Many newly freed women came to America as ladies' maids or as members of the large and varied entourages that customarily accompanied wealthy families emigrating to the colonies. Such was the position of Quiteria Gómez, a former slave, who with three other servants— one white male and two white females—traveled with the widow Francisca de Carrera and her seven children to Peru during 1555. Doña Francisca's two sisters made up the rest of the party, fourteen persons in all.

On the other hand, not all the Negroes who crossed the Atlantic went westward. In the second half of the sixteenth century there was a countermigration of Negroes from the

New World to Seville. Many Spaniards, having enriched themselves in America during the first decades of the sixteenth century, eventually returned home and took up residence in Seville, where they could maintain their contacts, usually commercial, with the Indies. These returning Spaniards, nicknamed *"indianos,"* invested their newly found wealth in elegant town houses, staffed with Negro slaves from the colonies. Don Álvaro in Castillo Solórzano's novel *La niña de los embustes—Teresa de Manzanares* was a typical *indiano* who, with 50,000 ducats obtained in Lima, two white servant boys, and four Negroes, established himself in Seville, spending his days at the Casa de Contratación. Creole slaves, as the Negroes from the colonies were called, also served in the homes of wealthy Sevillian merchants who were engaged in the trade with the Indies. The witty and attractive creole slave Elvira in Lope de Vega's *Servir a señor discreto* was the maid and confidante of Doña Leonor, the daughter of such a New World trader. The charm and beauty of the creole slave women soon made them a solicited commodity in the Sevillian slave market, as can be seen from the numerous deeds of purchase and sale which appear among the Sevillian Protocols. In 1580, for example, Diego de la Sal, a Sevillian aristocrat who traded with the New World, purchased a "twenty year old creole slave named Isabel de García" from a returning Spaniard. In time many of these creole slaves obtained their freedom either through purchase or the death of their owners, after which they sought to return to America. This accounts for the numerous references to them as passengers to the New World in the Casa registers during the last quarter of the sixteenth century.

Negro slaves and freedmen left many marks on Sevillian life of the sixteenth century. Whereas Moors and Moriscos remained on the fringes of Sevillian society, isolated and disliked by all, Negroes and mulattoes freely accepted Christianity and Spanish culture. As a result, they were eventually incorporated into the economic, social, and religious life of the city. When contemporary writers introduced Negro characters into their plays and novels, they only reflected the significant place that freedmen and slaves held in their society. The ethnic variety that characterized sixteenth-century Seville set it apart from other Spanish centers and increased its similarity to the cities of the New World. To this ethnic variety the Negro made a unique contribution.

5

CHARLES JULIAN BISHKO

THE INHERITANCE
OF THE PLAINSMAN

*Of the various institutional complexes that spread
from medieval Iberia to the New World, ranching was
of primary importance. Dominating the life during
colonial times of large sections of present-day Mexico,
Brazil, and Argentina, the cowboy and the rancher
have left many influences of their way of life throughout Latin America. In the following selection, Professor Bishko skillfully traces numerous elements
characteristic of Latin American ranching back to
their origins in medieval Spain.*

*Born in 1906, Charles Julian Bishko took his Ph.D.
from Harvard in medieval Spanish history. He first
taught at Radcliffe College and then at the University
of Virginia, where he is now Professor of History. He
has specialized in the history of medieval Iberian
monasticism and ranching and is the author of numerous important studies in these fields, published
both in American and foreign historical journals.*

From Charles Julian Bishko, "The Peninsular Background of
Latin American Cattle Ranching," *The Hispanic American
Historical Review*, XXXII (1952), 491–515. Reprinted by per-
mission of *The Hispanic American Historical Review*.

I

. . . like so many other features of Iberian civilization,
cattle ranching in the Middle Ages was virtually peculiar to
the Peninsula, a *cosa de España*. Cattle were, of course,
raised almost everywhere in medieval Europe, for their
dairy products—milk, cheese, butter; as draft animals—the
indispensable ox; and for their meat, tallow, and hides. But
such cattle were either a strictly subordinate element in
manorial crop agriculture, in which peasants might own at
best a few cows and a yoke or two of oxen; or they were
bred, e.g., in certain parts of Normandy, Wales and Ireland, on small dairy or feeder farms. In the medieval
Peninsula, cattle raising of these two types was widely
distributed, but most strongly established in what might be
called the Iberian Humid Crescent—the rainy, fertile crop
and grasslands that stretch from Beira in central Portugal
up through Galicia, swing east across the Cantabrian and
Pyrenean valleys, with certain southern salients like the
Leonese Tierra de Campos, the *comarca* of Burgos and the
Rioja Alta, and finally turn south into Catalonia. Throughout this region nobles, peasants, churches and monasteries
raised considerable stock on the basis of small herds
(*greyes*) averaging twenty to thirty head. These humid-
zone cattle belonged to still surviving northern Iberian
razas: Gallegas, Minhotas, Barrosãs, Arouquesas and
Mirandesas in Galicia, Minho, Trás-os-Montes and Beira
Alta; Asturianas in the Cantabrians; and various sub-
breeds of *Pirenáicas* between the Basque Provinces and the
Mediterranean. In color they ran predominantly to solid or
mixed shades of white, cream, dun, yellow and the lighter
and medium reds and browns; and they were in general
docile, easily handled and admirably suited to dairy, beef,
and draft needs.

But the raising of cattle on dairy or stock farms, or as a
subsidiary to dirt-farming, is not ranching, which implies

the ranging of cattle in considerable numbers over extensive grazing grounds for the primary purpose of large-scale production of beef and hides. With the possible exception of the Hungarian Plain and western portions of the British Isles, for both of which areas we badly need careful pastoral studies, medieval Iberia appears to have been the only part, as it was unquestionably the most important part, of medieval Europe to advance to this third level of cattle raising. While the precise circumstances must remain obscure, the available charters and *fueros* enable us to determine that a genuine ranch cattle industry evolved in the Peninsula in the late eleventh and twelfth centuries, under Alfonso VI and Alfonso VII of León-Castile. Its birthplace was not the Humid Crescent, but that portion of the subhumid or arid interior tableland of the Meseta Central lying between the middle course of the Duero River and the massive sierras of Gata, Gredos, and Guadarrama; or, more specifically, the *tierras* of Zamora and Salamanca in León, and those of Segovia and Avila in southern Old Castile.

From this original area of its nativity cattle ranching, on an ever increasing scale, expanded southward in the van of *reconquista* colonization. By the later twelfth century it had moved, along with the sheep industry of León, Castile and Portugal, into the broad pasturelands of New Castile, Extremadura and Alentejo, the latter region apparently being the cradle of the Portuguese ranching system, which was later extended into Algarve, the Atlantic Islands and the Brazilian *sertão*. On this southern half of the *meseta*, chiefly to the west of a line running through central New Castile, Castilian and Portuguese military orders, nobles and townsmen grazed thousands of cattle, although in both numbers and economic importance these were less significant than the great sheep flocks of the Mesta and other owners. But this situation was reversed after 1250, with Ferdinand III's reconquest of Andalusia, when royal *repartimientos* assigned to cattlemen rather than to sheep raisers the bulk of the *campos, campiñas* and *marismas* of the Guadalquivir valley. As a result, the Andalusian plain became in the latter Middle Ages the one region of the Peninsula, and perhaps of all Europe, where pastoral life, and indeed agricultural life in general, was dominated by a thriving, highly organized cattle-ranching economy. The fact that many of the early colonists of the Canaries and the Indies came from this Andalusian cattle kingdom, which was at its height in the fifteenth and early sixteenth centuries, or from the not too dissimilar cattle *ambiente* of Extremadura, provides one significant clue to the promotion of cattle over sheep ranching in the American colonies.

Just why medieval Castile and Portuguese Alentejo became the site of this widespread ranch cattle industry is a complex question. The only factor usually mentioned, the taking over or imitation of an already established Moorish cattle-ranching system, is clearly of secondary consequence. Some Moorish influence there undoubtedly was, especially in Andalusia, but the Berber was not much of a cattleman in North Africa, nor did he abandon in the Peninsula his typically Mediterranean preference for mutton over beef. Comparatively little in the techniques, vocabulary, dress or equipment of the Castilian and Portuguese cowboy can be traced to Moorish sources; and it is significant that the predominance of the old Iberian breeds of cattle was not adversely affected by African strains, as happened after the Moorish importation of the merino sheep and the Barb horse.

The really decisive factors determining the development of medieval Iberian cattle ranching appear to have been four in number, all of them native to the Peninsula:

(1) the presence, as in almost every phase of medieval Luso-Hispanic life, of numerous active, enterprising and ambitious individuals, many of whom were already familiar with Humid Crescent pastoralism and swiftly realized the broader opportunities presented by the conquest of the

meseta grazing grounds. Whether nobles, churchmen or town-dwelling *ganaderos,* such men were the first true prototypes of the cattle ranchers of the Indies.

(2) the transformation imposed upon Castilian and Portuguese agriculture by the frontier advance from northern, rainy, good-soiled "European" conditions onto the interior subhumid plains of the *meseta* . . . with their scarcity of water, poor soils and predominantly *mattoral*-type bush vegetation (the *monte bajo* of the stockman)— an environmental change that affected medieval Iberian life as radically as, in W. P. Webb's view, occupation of the Great Plains did American. Extremes of aridity and deficiencies of browse restricted cattle ranching chiefly to the western half of the *meseta;* Aragon was always strong sheep country, and in eastern New Castile, i.e., La Mancha, cattlemen were relatively few.

(3) the *Reconquista,* which for centuries created frontier areas on the *meseta* where Christians and Moors often raided or fought; where the population huddled in large, widely spaced towns separated by *despoblados;* where rural labor was scarce and crop-farming hazardous; and where cattle and sheep, being mobile and little demanding, had obvious advantages. Royal colonization policies, with their predilection for large seignorial and municipal grants, further accentuated pastoral trends.

(4) the special breed of cattle that developed on the *meseta* and the Andalusian Plain, cattle unique in medieval Europe. Moorish strains, as already observed, never became prominent; some North-African stock was brought in, but these were, as the reference to them in Cabeza de Vaca shows, the brown Atlas shorthorns still found in Morocco, and not to be confused with the native breeds of the Peninsula.

The cattle of Castilian and Portuguese ranching were— as nearly as a very amateur zootechnician can determine— the result of various degrees of crossing between lighter-colored European types of all-purpose cow found in the

Humid Crescent, and the wild, or semi-wild, black, dark red, and dark brown descendents of that uniquely Iberian strain, *Bos taurus ibericus,* the ancestor of the modern fighting bull. Mingling upon the *meseta* as the *reconquista* frontier drove southward, these two *razas* produced a very hardy hybrid stock, varying astonishingly in color and color combinations from creams, yellows and duns to deep browns, reds and blacks—a stock characterized by markedly feral instincts and often complete wildness. Such cattle were valuable chiefly for their tough hides and stringy beef. Medieval Castilians, however, were proud of them. The *Siete Partidas* notes with satisfaction that animals born in the hot frontier country were larger and stronger than those of the humid region; one fifteenth century writer, Fernando de la Torre, calls Castile the *"tierra de bravos toros";* another claims for her *"los mas grandes y mejores toros del mundo."* These cattle, unsuited for dairy or draft purposes, compelled the *criaderos, charros* and *serranos* of Castile and Portugal to abandon their cosy little cowpastures for the open range, to take to the horse for herding, to perfect systematic methods of long-distance grazing, periodical round-ups, branding, overland drives, and so forth—in short, to invent cattle ranching. These too are the cows whose long, stern faces, low-swinging heads, formidable horns, narrow sides and long legs appear on the opening pages of the family photograph albums of nearly every *criollo* breed of the Americas from the longhorns of the pampas to the longhorns of Texas.

These range cattle of the *meseta* and Andalusian Plain gave rise to a characteristic Iberian and, later, Ibero-American phenomenon, the *ganado bravo* or unbranded wild cattle existing in some numbers on the fringes of the ranching industry as a result of loose herding methods and the frontier conditions of the cattle country. The coexistence of herded, branded cows and wild, ownerless ones was a regular feature of peninsular *ganadería vacuna* long before there appeared across the ocean the very much larger wild herds of Española, New Spain, Brazil, the River Plate, and other regions; just as the medieval hunts of *ganado bravo* by mounted hunters, using dogs and armed with lances and pikes, anticipated the great *monterías* and *vaquerías* of Cuba, Española and the pampas.

From this same cattle background arose the *fiesta brava,* the bullfight, a prominent element in Iberian and Ibero-American social history that has too long been left to amateur historians. Much imaginative nonsense has been written about the alleged Roman or Moorish origins of the bullfight; but if one relies solely on historical evidence it seems highly probable that *toreo* first developed in the cattle *ambiente* of the *meseta* in the twelfth and thirteenth centuries. To this day the *suerte de picar* and the *suerte de banderillear* display old traditional techniques of handling and hunting range cattle, and the still archaic organization of bull raising and the *corrida* illumines certain otherwise obscure aspects of medieval ranching. For the intimate relationship existing in the Iberian mind between cow-punching, *ganado bravo,* and the bullfight, no better example can be cited than the familiar descriptions of the discovery of the buffalo in Cabeza de Vaca, Oñate, Villagrá, Castañeda, and others, passages whose strong ranching, cowhunting, and bullfighting flavor has never been fully appreciated. When, on the Great Plains of North America, as absolutely nowhere else in the Western hemisphere, Castilians encountered animals resembling cows, they naturally looked upon them as the *ganado bravo* declared by the *Siete Partidas* to be in the public domain. Despite certain visible evidence to the contrary, it followed that these animals must be ferocious, long-horned, risky to approach and, like difficult *toros de lidia,* given to attacking from the side and exceedingly dangerous to horses. Doubtless someone dismounted to try a *verónica* with his cape. In any case, the Plains Indians were obviously *vaqueros* who were already engaged in *vaquerías* which, if under Castilian management, would furnish hides for a lucrative trade.

II

In the sixteenth century not only the cow but the organization, methods and customs of the peninsular ranching system reached the Indies, there to become the enduring foundation of Latin-American ranching to the present day, the trunk from which have stemmed the various regional traditions that distinguish Mexican cattle techniques from Argentine, or Brazilian from Venezuelan. What was the nature of these parent institutions?

The ecological and frontier conditions of the *reconquista*, together with the steady demand for beef and hides, produced in portions of medieval Castile and Alentejo a fairly numerous class of cattle ranchers, although only in Andalusia did these outnumber the ubiquitous sheepmen. Of these peninsular cowmen a small but powerful seignorial group were large operators, with herds (*cabañas, hatos*) running up to a thousand or more head. Such, for example was the rancher-noble Don Juan Alfonso de Benavides, who *ca.* 1306 ranged up to around 800 cows; or the Castilian Dominican nunneries of Santo Domingo de Caleruega, Santo Domingo de Madrid and Santa Clara de Guadalajara, with 1000, 1500, and 1000 head, respectively. The military orders of Castile and Portugal also belonged to this group, with their extensive ranges held as *encomiendas* in New Castile, Andalusia, Alentejo and Algarve. In 1302, the Castilian branch at Uclés of the Order of Santiago had at least a thousand head, while the Orders of Santiago de León and of Calatrava found it necessary to appoint special administrative officials for their great herds, the *comendadores de las vacas,* who were subject to supervision by *visitadores.* The figures just cited of 800, 1000, and 1500 represent the known maximum herd sizes for the Peninsula before 1500 and lie back of the amusing passages in Oviedo's *Historia general y natural de las Indias* (III, 11; XII, 9), where that writer astonishes his readers with herds in the Caribbean area running to five, ten, twenty thousand or more cows.

Most peninsular cattlemen, however, had much smaller holdings than the wealthier magnates and ecclesiastical corporations. Even among nobles and monasteries were many, like the Premonstratensian house of Nuestra Señora de la Vid, which in 1292 owned 4000 sheep and only 200 cows, for whom cattle ranching was a relatively minor interest. But the great majority of medieval *ganaderos* in the cattle business were *vecinos* of the towns, whose herds rarely exceeded a few hundred head and often ran very much lower. In thirteenth and fourteenth century New Castile, for example, the royal *privilegios* establish three categories of municipal cowmen: those with under 40 head; those owning 40 to 100; and those with above 100. Yet it is essential to recognize that these *dueños de ganado,* for all their small herds, were not mere stockfarmers of Humid Crescent type; their cattle grazed not on small farms but great municipal ranges and were often driven long distances for seasonal pasturage; and small *vacadas* were frequently combined on an *aparcería* basis into larger herds, the *aparceros* thus becoming partners in an enterprise of some size. Furthermore, in the fourteenth and fifteenth centuries, notably in Extremadura and Andalusia, the *vecinos* owning over 100 cows increased markedly in number and in the size of their herds. The *fueros* of Cáceres and Usagre set a minimum of 400 cows for pasturage drives northward, thus compelling *vecinos* to form *aparcerías* of this scale; and *ca.* 1491 Málaga found it impossible to enforce a 150 head limit for grazing on its ranges. The *cabildo* of Seville in 1493 defined an *hato de vacas* as consisting of as many as 500 cattle, and even allowed for larger herds in the hands of its citizens, some of whom evidently ran stock on their own *dehesas, montes, prados* and *pastos* as well as on the municipal ranges.

Recognition of the dividing line between municipal and seignorial cattle ranching in medieval Iberia is basic to its proper understanding. The distinction finds reflection not merely in disparity of size between town ranching outfits and those of the nobles, monasteries and military orders at the top of the industry, but in differences of organization, land use and pasturage and marketing rights. Seignorial ranching operated far more freely than municipal, which partly explains why the *cabildos* of the Indies had so much difficulty imposing livestock controls upon the new colonial landed classes. While abundant data on *vaqueros'* wages and the prices of hides, leather and meat can be found in the *cuadernos* of the medieval Castilian and Portuguese Cortes, neither these nor the royal law codes contain any considerable body of restrictive legislation aimed at close control of seignorial cattle ranching. It is not necessary to review the history of medieval Iberian grazing rights, stock taxes and royal transhumancy laws, so definitely treated for Castile by Klein, although we still lack a comparable study for Portugal; such regulations of course affected seignorial ranchers. It is however significant to note that the great Castilian cattlemen never organized, either voluntarily or under royal compulsion, a counterpart to the sheepmen's Real Consejo de la Mesta, even though in Extremadura and Andalusia their struggle over pasturage with that powerful national gild must have suggested the advantages of union and royal support. Very likely the Mesta itself opposed any inclination of the Castilian kings from Alfonso X on to charter a parallel society of cattle raisers; and perhaps the inclusion of some cattle owners in the Mesta, as attested by its documents and by the bull prominently displayed alongside the merino sheep on its coat-of-arms, reflects an unsuccessful attempt to win over seignorial cattlemen into a kind of national stockmen's association.

Municipal ranchers, on the other hand, were rigorously supervised by the local town government, the *concejo* or *concelho,* which controlled their grazing grounds. The later medieval *fueros* and ordinances of Castilian and Alentejan towns regulate almost every aspect of cattle ranching: grazing rights; compensations for crop damage; wages of cowboys; branding; penalties for rustling, brand-changing, or killing another man's stock; marketing and sale of cattle in the town's markets, butchershops and *ferias;* slaughtering practices; and many other related subjects. Some towns, although clearly not all, possessed a stockmen's gild or *mesta,* which operated as a kind of municipal bureau of pastoral affairs, and must be carefully distinguished from the national Mesta Real of the transhumant sheepmen. Jurisdiction of the local *mesta* was confined to the town's *términos;* all *vecinos* grazing cattle, sheep, horses, goats, pigs, and other animals on the municipal ranges were required to join, while strenuous efforts were made to impose membership upon non-*vecinos* holding pasturelands adjacent to those of the town. While subordinate to the supreme authority of the *concejo,* such local *mestas,* which held meetings two or three times a year under their elected *alcaldes de la mesta,* were powerful bodies, administering all the livestock provisions of the local law code. In the cattle country, these *mestas* at times subdivided along the lines of *ganado mayor* and *menor;* this meant that the local cowmen had their own organization, a kind of sub-*mesta,* under their own duly elected *alcalde* or *alcaldes de la mesta,* who fined or otherwise punished violaters of cattle laws and settled disputes among the ranchers. A major function of municipal *mestas* was to regulate and protect the use of brands and earmarks, and to facilitate recovery of lost cattle. Cattlemen were commonly required to work their herds in the spring and fall for all stray stock (*mesteños, mostrencos*) and turn these over to the *mesta* officials. The latter, after recording the brands and other distinguishing features of the strays, and having the *pregón* or crier proclaim these details at intervals in the plaza mayor, held the animals for a fixed period of months in a corral pending identification by the owners. The best and most colorful picture we have of such a local *mesta* connected with a genuine cowtown is contained in the 1527 *Ordenanças* of Seville, which describe in detail the old semi-annual meetings of the ranchers outside the Hospital de los

Criaderos in the Calle de Arrayán. Here in the open air, amid the dust of *dueños de ganado* and *mayorales* galloping in from the *campo,* while *mesteños* turned into the nearby corral bawled their protests, the *alcalde de la mesta* heard *pleitos,* administered justice, settled quarrels, and supervised his *escribano* in the registration of brands in the official *libro de la mesta.* These Seville *alcaldes de la mesta,* like those of sixteenth-century Mexico City, also traveled on circuit to district *mestas* in more remote parts of the municipal territory.

In other towns of the cattle country, however, no trace of a municipal *mesta* can be found in the *fueros* or *ordenanzas;* here the *concejo* or *concelho* itself administered pastoral affairs, and its own *alcaldes* and their *escribano* performed the functions elsewhere assigned to the *mesta* officials. This appears to have been the precedent generally followed in the Americas, where, from the sixteenth century on, *cabildos* like those of Lima, Caracas, Habana, and many others exercised direct control over the ranch cattle industry, as their *actas capitulares* testify. In Mexico City, however, an important exception occurs; here, in 1537, under order of Charles V and Viceroy Mendoza, the *cabildo* organized a *mesta* for handling livestock problems, which deserves further study. Recent writers have regarded its establishment as marking the introduction into New Spain of the Real Concejo de la Mesta, but its creation by, and subjection to, the *cabildo,* its municipal membership, and the general character of its organization and aims, indicate that it was closer to a municipal *mesta* of Andalusian type adapted to New World conditions than a colonial counterpart of the national Mesta of the Castilian transhumant sheep industry.

As for the cowboys themselves, only the briefest mention of questions requiring further examination can be made. Their life, and that of the cowgirls as well, finds its most vivid memorial in the fourteenth century picaresque poem of Juan Ruiz, archpriest of Hita; students have yet to recognize how thoroughly this masterpiece of medieval

Castilian literature reflects the life of the range cattle country between Segovia and Toledo. In the municipal sources, these medieval ancestors of the *vaqueros, vaqueiros, gauchos, huasos* and *llaneros* of the Indies always appear as freemen, who hire themselves out for a year's time, usually from one *día de San Juan* to the next, and receive an annual wage (*soldada*) paid in cash, a percentage of calves, or a combination of these. Whether, as seems inherently likely, unfree cowboys could also be found, performing compulsory herding services for seignorial *dueños de ganado* like some *indios de encomienda* in the New World, is unknown. *Vaqueros* were held liable to deduction of pay for stock lost; in cases of rustling, sworn statements supported by other men of trust were required; and when an animal died, it was necessary to produce the hide and affirm under oath that the death was due to natural causes or the attacks of wolves or bears. When express permission was granted, the peninsular cowboy might graze a few cows, marked with his own brand, alongside those of his employer. The herds were not left to roam at will, but kept under standing guard to avoid both stock losses and the heavy penalties imposed for trespass against the *cinco cosas vedadas:* orchards, grain fields, vineyards, ox pastures and mown meadows. As with sheep, dogs were used to assist the vaqueros in guarding and on round-ups. Herds of any size were tended by a foreman (*mayoral, rabadán, mayordomo*) and from three to four *vaqueros* on up. Large outfits often had both a *mayoral* and *rabadán,* and perhaps a dozen or more hands. In Andalusia such crews normally included a *conocedor,* who memorized each cow's appearance as an aid in detecting strays or identifying the owner's own lost stock. Such a post could, of course, exist only where, as seen, cattle varied infinitely in color, and where also Spanish and Portuguese provided that remarkably rich, syncopated terminology of color and marking terms for cows and horses such as no other European language possesses. The *conocedor* clearly filled an important need in the period prior to official registration of brands, but the advent of the municipal *libro de marcas y señales* in the late fifteenth century soon ended his usefulness; although he can be found still flourishing in the 1527 *Ordenanças* of Seville, he does not appear to have crossed the ocean.

The dress and equipment of Latin-American cowmen owe much to peninsular models. Students of costume could doubtless trace back to the twelfth century regional dress of the *charros* and *serranos* of Salamanca and southern Old Castile, the cradle of the ranch cattle industry, the cowboy costume that appears with many local variations in the Indies: the low-crowned, broad-brimmed hat, the bolero jacket, the sash and tight-fitting trousers, the spurred boots. Since, for herding on the open range, mounted *vaqueros* were indispensable, the rise of Iberian cattle ranching could hardly have occurred if the Peninsula had not been in the Middle Ages the one European region where saddle horses were at once relatively abundant and cheap enough to escape being an aristocratic monopoly. Numerous references to horses and horse-breeding in the cattle documents indicate that the horse herd, the later *remuda* or *caballada*, was a normal feature of peninsular cowboy life, although much work remains to be done on the regional origins of the cowhorse, the evolution of saddle, bridle, stirrups and spurs, and the relative importance of the northern *silla de brida* and the Moorish *silla de ginete* riding styles, both of which appear among Latin-American cattlemen.

For working stock the Castilian and Alentejan *vaquero* carried the long pike-like *garrocha*, which still survives in peninsular ranching and bullfighting use, and can be found also among Venezuelan *llaneros*, Brazilian *sertanejos* and other American cowboys. Carrying of arms was strictly regulated by the *concejos* in an effort to check brawls, *vaqueros* being ordinarily forbidden to possess any other weapons than the *garrocha* and the *puñal pastoril*, perhaps a distant forerunner of the Bowie knife. That the *reata* or *lazo* was known in the Peninsula has been denied, but while it is impossible to decide, from the few known medieval references to ropes (*sogas*) used on cattle, whether or not these were noosed, the apparently early diffusion of the rawhide *reata,* with its remarkably complex techniques and vocabulary, throughout the New-World cattle industry points to an Iberian origin. In any case peninsular cowboys also handled *reses vacunos* with the *garrocha,* with the aid of trained, belled steers (*cabestros*) and by their dexterity in throwing animals to the ground with a twist of the tail or horns, all of which alternatives to roping are still used in Ibero-America.

For grazing purposes, cattle were ranged either as *estantes* in local pastures that often varied seasonally from lowland to nearby sierra; or as *transhumantes* that might be driven as much as 400 miles over the official trails or *cañadas* linking the summer pastures (*agostaderos*) of León and Castile with the winter *invernaderos* of the south. The proportion of migrant to nonmigrant herds is difficult to determine; cows were less transhumant than sheep, but even so large numbers were trailed each year *á los extremos,* over the same routes as the Mesta flocks. Royal charters granting towns and military orders along the *cañadas* the right to collect *montazgo* from the transhumants reckon this toll for units as high as 1000 and even 2000 cows. At certain seasons the collective trail herds of the towns, and others belonging to nobles, monasteries and military orders, must have marched along the *cañadas* in a great series, accompanied by their heavily armed cavalry escorts (the *rafalas*), and by *dueños* and *vaqueros* who doubtless entertained their charges by day with the profaner aspects of diverse Leonese and Castilian dialects, soothed them at night with renditions of secular and ecclesiastical songs—cf. the *vaquero* songs in the Arcipreste—and defended them from the perils of drought, storm, stampede and attack by Moorish or other foe. Yet, in many parts of the *meseta, reses estantes* predominated. In Andalusia long distance transhumancy seems to have consisted more · of northern herds moving in from the

meseta than of Guadalquivir valley ranchers trailing stock
north of the Sierra Morena. The *Ordenanças* of Seville,
which apply to all the many towns of its *tierra* as well as to
the capital itself, make no mention of the migrations so
carefully regulated in *fueros* such as those of Cáceres and
Usagre.

The traditional Latin-American cycle of ranching life,
with the rounding-up and branding of calves in the spring
herredero and the cutting-out of beef for slaughter in the
autumn, comes straight from peninsular practice. Miranda
. . . claims the *rodeo,* or round-up, as an *"institución
castizamente americana,"* but this is far from certain.
Municipal laws forced ranchers to work their herds at least
once, and commonly twice, a year in order to brand calves,
remove strays and cut out stock for market; although this
involved, strictly speaking, only each *criadero's* rounding
up his own cows, it is difficult to believe that some form of
cooperative *rodeo* had not emerged before 1500. But this
question must remain open until we have had further
research upon the whole history of the *rodeo,* its role in the
pastoral organization of the Indies, and the connection
between its *alcaldes* or *jueces del campo* (the round-up
bosses or captains of Texas) and the municipal *alcaldes de
la mesta.*

Branding is unquestionably a very ancient peninsular
livestock practice, dating from at least the Roman period.
The oldest medieval brand yet discovered is a heart-shaped
one depicted on the flanks of a bull and a horse in two
tenth-century manuscripts of the Leonese abbey of San
Miguel de Escalada. No study has yet been attempted of
peninsular cattle brands (*hierros, marcas*) or of the supplementary system of earcrops (*señales*), although it is
obvious that they are the immediate prototypes of the
intricate symbols and monograms common to Latin-
American and Anglo-American ranching. Branding was
originally optional in the Peninsula, being used by the
stockmen for their own protection, but from at least the
thirteenth century the *fueros* require it of all municipal

ranchers. The brand book, destined to become universal in the Americas, is a comparatively late device; down to the fifteenth century the *concejos* kept simply a temporary record of the brands of strays turned into the town corral. Only in the latter part of that century do we find evidence that at least in Andalusia some towns were compelling the cattlemen of their *tierra* to register brands and earmarks with the town or *mesta escribano*, by whom they were inscribed in a genuine brand register, the *libro de marcas y señales* or *libro de la mesta*. The relative novelty of the *libro de marcas* may help explain why in New Spain, New Castile and elsewhere *cabildos* and royal officials encountered so much difficulty in getting *ganaderos* to register brands or even to brand at all. Whether any peninsular brand book of the Middle Ages still exists in some unsearched archive is unknown, but probable enough; at present the oldest known such register for the entire Luso-Hispanic and Ibero-American world seems to be the remarkable *Relación de los hierros de bacas y obejas y bestias,* which the cabildo of Mexico City opened in 1530, seven years before it established the New Spanish *mesta*.

A final question of prime importance for colonial agrarian institutions is that of the peninsular or American origin of the cattle ranch, variously styled in the Indies *sitio de ganado mayor, hacienda de ganado, fazenda, finca, hato, sitio de estancia, estancia* and the like. From the fact that throughout the Middle Ages royal pasturage rights in *realengo* land were conceded by the Castilian and Portuguese crowns to towns, nobles and ecclesiastical corporations, and by them granted or rented to their *vecinos,* vassals or others, it has been contended that ranching based upon private ownership of large estates was a New World invention. The subject is too involved for more than brief mention here, but it should be noted that this view rests solely upon documents dealing with transhumancy and municipal ranching, fields in which rights would naturally loom larger than land titles. Yet evidence that seignorial ranchers frequently possessed extensive domains that were in effect true *estancias* is readily discoverable. The *pergaminos* of Madrid mention privately owned grazing grounds in New Castile, while those of Cáceres reveal that in late medieval Extremadura private pasturelands were threatening to absorb, by purchase or usurpation, the communal ranges of towns and villages. The military orders held great *dehesas* in Extremadura, New Castile and Andalusia, some of which they grazed directly, while others were allotted to their stock-raising vassals. The Seville *Ordenanças* cite *campiñas, cortijos, casas fuertes, donadíos* and other large *heredades,* located in the *marismas* and *islas* of the Guadalquivir, from which the municipal herds were barred and which were evidently being operated as seignorial ranches. Even among municipal ranchers there were those who in addition to grazing cattle on town lands had their own *dehesas, dehesas dehesadas, prados, sotos* and *pastos,* some of which were certainly larger than mere cowpastures. It is noteworthy that *ca.* 1500, probably in response to seignorial influence, some Castilian and Andalusian towns, instead of allowing, as previously, unrestricted movement of herds within their *términos,* were siting (*asentar*) *reses estantes* on assigned portions of their *tierra;* this trend toward municipal allocation of grazing sites may have given rise in the Indies to the term *estancia* (commonly classified as an Americanism) and to the grants of *sitio de ganado, sitio de estancia,* etc., for which a municipal origin may be conjectured.

Even in our present state of knowledge regarding the development of *latifundismo* in late medieval Spain and Portugal, it seems possible to reach two principal conclusions about the *estancia.* The first is that by the fourteenth and fifteenth centuries the ranch (i.e., the seignorial estate devoted to large-scale stockraising) and the landed *ganadero* were both well established in the peninsular cattle kingdom, probably to a much greater extent than in the more heavily transhumant sheep industry upon which alone previous judgments have been based. The second conclusion is that not only was peninsular ranching thus characterized *ca.* 1500 by a dual system of pasturage rights and large landed estates, but that the system was in a state of flux, with the domanial element in the ascendent. It is this dualism, in process of transition from rights to tenures, that finds reflection in sixteenth-century colonial documents. In New Spain, New Castile, and the Brazilian *capitanias,* as in Iberia, grazing rights in royal and municipal land coexisted with *sitios de ganado, tierras de señorío* and *fazendas.* The seignorial *estancia* triumphed early under New-World conditions of conquest and settlement, but, like so many other elements in the Ibero-American cattle tradition, it was almost certainly an importation from the Peninsula.

III

That the ranch cattle industry of Castile and Alentejo expanded between 1200 and 1500 in both territorial extent and volume of production, in response to incresing demand for beef and hides, is a safe inference, but nearly all aspects of this process have been neglected by historians. Marketing centered about the towns, especially the great cattle fairs (*ferias de ganado, ferias de gado*) that were held annually by old cowtowns like Segovia, Avila, Plasencia, Béjar, Cáceres, Córdoba, Seville, Evora, Beja and others. At these, local slaughterers competed with professional itinerant cattle buyers, who traveled from one town to another and drove their purchases north to markets or feeding grounds outside the cattle country. Galicia, already in the Middle Ages what she remains to this day—Spain's chief milch cow center—was also, it would seem, an important beef feeder region for *meseta* cattle, like present-day western Buenos Aires and eastern La Pampa provinces, southern Brazil or the northern Great Plains of the

United States. Hamilton's statistics suggest that prices on beef, hides, tallow, and other cattle products rose markedly in the fourteenth and fifteenth centuries, in line with the price structure as a whole. To a degree unusual in the cereal-consuming Middle Ages, meat, whether fresh, salted, or dried (*carne seca*), was a staple foodstuff for Spaniards and inland Portuguese, a fact which explains another curious Iberian and Ibero-American phenomenon, the Bula de la Cruzada, with its virtual repeal of the dietary meat restrictions of medieval Catholic Europe.

As for hides, their mounting output can be linked to the significant late medieval shift of the peninsular tanning and leather trades from goat and sheep skins, which the Moors had preferred for their Córdoban and Moroccan leathers, to the tougher, if less workable, cowhide. From the limited data thus far assembled on this subject, it looks as if cowhides were not only in heavy demand at home but were also the basis of an important export trade to Italy, France, the Low Countries, and perhaps other areas. Furthermore, this does not imply a surplus, for in late medieval Andalusia hides were being imported from North Africa, England, Ireland and, within the Peninsula itself, from dairy-farming Galicia and other districts. Presumably this means that peninsular hide production *ca.* 1500 was insufficient to satisfy home and export demands; if so, this enables us to grasp the immediate economic circumstances under which colonial Latin-American cattle raising and early large-scale export of cowhides from the colonies first developed.

The demands of the home market, mercantilist preference for colonial rather than foreign sources of raw material, the colonists' own need for a commodity yielding quick overseas revenues, and the natural disinclination of the Crown and the Real Concejo de la Mesta to foster a competitive wool industry in the Indies, must all have combined to swing the New World decision to the cow instead of the sheep. To be sure, sheep raising was by no means neglected; in New Spain, for example, Viceroy

Mendoza encouraged it strongly, and in Peru, as Cieza de León's frequent references indicate, large numbers of imported Iberian sheep along with the native llamas dominated the livestock picture. Yet this colonial wool seems to have been almost wholly intended for local use and not for export to the Peninsula, where the Mesta successfully protected its markets against colonial competition. What effect the rise of a far more productive American cattle industry had upon the eventual decline of peninsular cattle ranching, and to what extent this decline contributed to insuring the complete triumph of the Spanish sheepmen in the Hapsburg period, are interesting questions to which no answer is now possible.

Such, in broad and tentative outline, is the peninsular background of Latin-American cattle ranching. To students of colonial and modern Latin America it should not seem altogether unfamiliar. Changes there certainly were in the organization of the industry when it crossed the ocean; but the coexistence of seignorial and municipal ranching; their common conflict with the agriculturist, whether *encomendero* or Indian; the regulatory activities of government, both royal and municipal, in connection with pasturage, branding, marketing and the like; the commerce in hides; the traditional cycle of the cowman's year; above all, the *ganaderos* and *vaqueros* themselves, galloping along in the dust of their wild or half-wild herds—these are the stuff of colonial and post-colonial ranching no less than of that of the Peninsula. In the New World a vaster cattle kingdom was founded, but, as every reader of *Os Sertões* and *Doña Bárbara* discovers, it continued to preserve tenaciously its traditional institutions, many of which still flourish. It was with a cattle country in mind, and in words that apply to many other stockraising regions of the Western Hemisphere, that Sarmiento declared in *Facundo* (chap. ii): *"En la República Argentina se ven a un tiempo dos civilizaciones distintas en un mismo suelo. . . . El siglo xix y el siglo xii viven juntos; el uno dentro de las ciudades, el otro en las campañas.*"[1] No more perfectly expressed estimate could be made of the enduring influence of medieval Iberian cattle ranching upon the history of the Americas.

---

[1] "In the Argentine Republic, one sees, at one and the same time, two distinct civilizations on the same ground. . . . The nineteenth century and the twelfth live side by side; the one in the cities, the other in the countryside." (Ed.)

6

ROBERT S. CHAMBERLAIN

THE ROOTS OF LORDSHIP: THE *ENCOMIENDA* IN MEDIEVAL CASTILE

Brought by the conquistadors to the New World, many medieval Castilian institutions soon underwent a quasi-biological transformation. Freed from the peninsular system of checks and balances that had made them regulated parts of a social whole, they suddenly burgeoned and expanded in the new environment where few of the old countervailing forces existed. Certainly such was the case with the encomienda. In the following selection, Robert S. Chamberlain describes the institution in its complex medieval setting, where it formed merely one among many of the different types of lordship that had grown up in the period of the Reconquest. All of these were undergoing a process of increasing royal control during the later fifteenth century. His account should

From Robert S. Chamberlain, "Castilian Backgrounds of the *Repartimiento-Encomienda,*" *Carnegie Institution of Washington: Contributions to American Anthropology and History,* V (1939), 33–52. Reprinted by permission of the Carnegie Institution of Washington.

make it easier for the student to understand the reasons for royal opposition to the unregulated spread of encomienda *in the New World, where it threatened to recreate across the Atlantic another "overmighty" nobility of the kind that Ferdinand and Isabella had just managed to subdue at home.*

Born in 1903, Robert S. Chamberlain received his doctorate from Harvard in 1936 and, from then until 1948, served as a staff member of the Historical Research Division of the Carnegie Institution of Washington. Since 1948, Dr. Chamberlain has been with the United States Government. Among his more important publications are The Conquest and Colonization of Yucatan *and* The Governorship of Adelantado Francisco de Montejo in Chiapas, 1539–1544.

During the Middle Ages and the Renaissance the kings of the realms of Castile, . . . to consummate their policies and to provide reward for services, made grants of territory, cities, towns, lands, castles, revenues, and privileges to the nobles, prelates and churches, abbots and monasteries, and the military orders and their authorities. These donations and grants were, in the broader sense, comparable to those made by sovereigns of the other states of Western Europe and they had their origin in needs and conditions which were, in the ultimate analysis, fundamentally similar to those which existed elsewhere. As was the practice in other realms, the nobles, bishops, churches, abbots, monasteries, and the military orders and their officials also made grants and donations.

The conquest of the Iberian Peninsula by the Moors and the Reconquista, which were major factors in determining the course of the history of Castile from the first years of the eighth century until the close of the fifteenth, to a great degree conditioned the form of the donations and grants made within those realms and tended to impart to them a specialized character, although, as indicated, their basic nature and purpose were the same as those of donations and grants given in other states of Europe. Moreover, absorbed in the Reconquista, relations with neighboring kingdoms of the Iberian Peninsula, and her own internal problems, Castile developed in relative isolation from the countries north of the Pyrenees. Castilian institutions, consequently, were not greatly influenced by developments elsewhere. While influences from the outside were not totally absent, such as did exist were transformed or sublimated.

During the long period of the Reconquista it was necessary for the Castilian monarchs and their principal vassals to conduct virtually constant warfare, to repeople conquered territory, to people uninhabited areas, to organize the lands acquired administratively, and to provide for effective military defence. At the same time, the kings of Castile were required to face the problems arising from the government of lands long held, internal strife, and wars with other Christian Kingdoms of the peninsula, which also necessitated the giving of grants and donations. These circumstances determined the form and character of the donations and grants which came into existence, and they consequently had as their purpose the establishment and maintenance of government, the provision of military defense, the peopling or repeopling of lands conquered, the rewarding of services, and the establishment of the obligations of fealty and continued service.

The donations and grants made in Castile by the sovereigns, lay and spiritual lords, churches and monasteries, and the military orders and their authorities assumed various forms and were given with widely varying conditions with respect to jurisdiction, territorial status, and length of tenure. They existed under the designations *prestimonio, mandación, encomienda, feudo, tenencia, tierra, heredad,* and *honor.* . . . All were made through formal titles and diplomas and involved recognition by the vassal of the dominion of the overlord and the obligation that the former serve the latter. The obligation of military service was definitely asserted in certain instances and was implicit in others, and the majority of grants and donations were accompanied by a *pleito-homenaje*[1] on the part of the recipient and a ceremony of investiture. The institutions and usages themselves became an integral part of the structure of society in Castile, which, as already indicated, may be termed Castilian feudalism, or a seignorial regime.

.   .   .

Important among grants of early origin were those in *prestimonio* (*proestimonium, prestimonium, prestación, préstamo*), in *encomienda* (*commissum, commenda, comienda*), and in *mandación* (*mandationem*). The prestimonio was a limited grant of jurisdiction over towns and territory, with the usufruct of the lands involved, in return for service. The grant was normally of lifetime duration, and the vassal was not empowered to alienate the land assigned, which upon expiration of the grant reverted to the overlord. The vassal received the tributes and services owed to the overlord by the inhabitants of the lands involved under fuero and usage, relinquishing to the latter a designated portion of the tributes. In giving grants in prestimonio the Crown at times retained certain elements of jurisdiction. Grants in prestimonio were given by churches and the hierarchy and monasteries and abbots in lands of *abadengo*, and the Church had more frequent recourse to this type of grant than did the Crown and lay lords. After the thirteenth century the sovereign and nobles appear not to have made grants under this title.

The encomienda and the mandación, originally by nature and purpose more restricted grants than the prestimonio, were assigned by the Crown to members of the royal family, magnates, *caballeros*, prelates, abbots, authorities of the military orders, churches, and monasteries

---

[1] A pledge of homage. (Ed.)

for purposes of administration, the peopling of territory, and the provision of defense, and in reward of services. When a *conde* was assigned a grant in ecomienda or in mandación the territory involved was known as a *condado,* the lord taking his title from the district given into his control. If the lord was not a conde he was known as the señor of the town or district granted to him. In the earlier period grants in encomienda and in mandación were very similar, if not identical, and it is difficult to distinguish between them on a juridical basis. Later, from about the twelfth century, they became differentiated with regard to powers and the conditions of acquisition.

The encomienda consisted in the temporary grant by the sovereign of territory, cities, towns, castles, and monasteries, with powers of government and the right to receive the revenues, or a stipulated part thereof, and the services owed to the Crown by the people of the areas concerned under fuero and custom. The grant was given for the lifetime of the recipient, for that of the sovereign, or at the will of the latter. In its jurisdictional aspect the encomienda was a charge of government, the comendador, or encomendero (*comendero*), exercising the authority of the Crown in the area involved, and in its territorial aspect it constituted a temporary patrimony. The comendador, or encomendero, possessed no power to change the status of the people of the lands assigned, nor to alter the established tributes and services.

Although encomiendas by essential nature were temporary grants, from the first the lords to whom they were assigned regarded them as patrimonies which should not be removed without just cause. Those given at the will of the sovereign tended to become lifetime grants in fact, and those for lifetime tended to become hereditary, frequently being transmitted from father to son by special *merced* of the Crown.

From the eleventh century the Church gave towns and *heredades* in encomienda to powerful nobles for the preservation and defense of holdings, such grants being necessary because of political anarchy and warfare which made it impossible for the Church to maintain order throughout her lands and prevent usurpation. The Church gave these grants with the same general conditions as did the Crown, but with more rigid specific stipulations. These, as similar royal grants, were at first temporary, but by custom became lifetime holdings, many being passed from father to son with the express consent of the churchman who was the señor of the territory.

·   ·   ·

From the fifteenth century the encomiendas granted by the Crown and the Church were gradually suppressed, only those of the military orders continuing to exist.

The mandación, like the encomienda, was originally a grant by virtue of which the king conferred upon the recipient all or a portion of his territorial, jurisdictional, and fiscal prerogatives over land, towns, and castles for a period dependent upon his will or for lifetime. The mandación was at times designated as such in the diploma of cession and at others was inferred by the phrase *ad imperandum*. As already noted, the powers of the grantee appear to have been much the same as those of recipients of grants in encomienda. Lords other than the sovereign and the Church also gave grants of this type.

Although temporary by original nature, the mandación tended to perpetuate itself in the same manner as did the encomienda. This was especially true in the case of mandaciones granted to churches and the hierarchy and monastic foundations and their officials, a tendency favored by the Crown through privileges accorded to the Church and orders permitting the acquisition of land by donation. Mandaciones which became perpetual became known as *señoríos*,[2] while those which remained temporary may have evolved into the type of grant designated as the

---

[2] Seigniory or lordship. (Ed.)

tenencia, although it is possible that the latter type of grant may have made its appearance independently.

. . .

From the first days of the Reconquista, and especially from the eleventh century, the Crown granted lands in territory regained from the Moors, which pertained to the sovereign in *dominio alodial*,[3] to those who participated in the conquest in recompense of services and to provide for the peopling, government, and defense of such territory. This practice became fixed custom, and to a certain degree was obligatory on the part of the sovereign, especially in view of the fact that the conquistadors served at their own *costa y misión*[4] and thus possessed added claims for compensation. When the Reconquista was extended to the rich area of Andalusia, the partition of lands was regularized as the institution of the *repartimiento*. Immediately upon conquest the territories acquired were divided among the greater and lesser nobles, prelates and churches, and the authorities of monastic foundations and the military orders. In this manner the areas of Jaén, Baeza, Córdoba, Sevilla, Jérez de la Frontera, and Murcia were partitioned, lands, towns, *aldeas, alquerías*,[5] and castles being assigned in the areas of these cities, and casas and plots being granted within their immediate limits. These grants included a certain number of towns and districts which the Moorish inhabitants had not abandoned. Grants in repartimiento were made in dominio alodial by *juro de heredad*,[6] being known as heredades, and imposed the *deber de milicia*, including the obligation of maintaining arms and a horse or of supporting a mounted or foot soldier, and a certain requirement of residence. Over and above the grants to the greater nobles, prelates and churches, and

---

[3] Land held in full ownership with no superior. (Ed.)

[4] Expense. (Ed.)

[5] Villages, hamlets. (Ed.)

[6] With right to bequeath to successors. (Ed.)

monastic foundations and the military orders, some three hundred caballeros were granted heredades in Baeza, two hundred in Seville, forty Jérez de la Frontera, and three hundred thirty-three in Murcia.

Grants of heredades made in repartimiento by juro de heredad were perpetual and irrevocable and the possessor enjoyed the right to transmit them by inheritance or to dispose of them by sale, exchange, or transfer. Such grants *ipso facto* conferred permanent señorío upon the recipient when they involved jurisdiction over people. From the grant of lands in repartimiento developed the great *latifundios* of the nobles in Andalusia, and as a result of the practice the Church and the religious and military orders also acquired extensive holdings. The repartimiento and assignment of lands was placed in effect in the areas of Málaga and Granada upon the conquest of the last Moorish kingdom at the close of the fifteenth century, and lands in the Canaries were assigned in repartimiento following the final conquest of those islands. The repartimientos were carried out and the assignments were made either directly by the sovereigns or by repartidores designated by them.

The military orders, which played an important role in the Reconquista, were by royal grants assigned lands, towns, castles, and vassals in areas conquered from the Moors for purposes of government and defense, especially in frontier areas, and in reward of services and to assure future support, and Moorish *caseríos* were placed under the protectorate of the masters. Places, *heredamientos*, and *rentas* were also acquired by the orders through donations by the Crown and nobles and through conquests which they themselves made from the Moors. The wide holdings of the orders in Andalusia were outstanding among their possessions.

The chapters of the orders, to permit them to fulfill their obligations and maintain the eminence of their position, assigned to the masters an increasing number of towns and castles and increased revenues. These were assigned with the specific obligations to maintain and repair churches, sustain worship, provide ornaments for churches, and maintain and repair castles and fortresses. Supreme powers of government in the lands of the orders were also conceded to the masters.

Encomiendas and *prioratos*[7] were created by the orders for administrative and military purposes and to reward the services of the worthy and older members and to sustain caballeros who enjoyed no *pensiones*. These encomiendas and prioratos were assigned by the masters. Encomiendas consisted of towns, castles, lands, and vassals and the grant carried jurisdiction over the territories and people involved. The recipient of an encomienda, or comendador, was under obligation to maintain a certain number of lances for military service, granting to these emoluments, to support the curas of the churches of the encomienda, and to give alms to the needy. The masters and comendadores granted fueros and *cartas-pueblas* to the towns of encomienda which established the status of the inhabitants and fixed the tributes and services.

In assuming the headship and supreme control of the military orders the Catholic Kings removed the dangers to royal authority inherent in such institutions and adopted means of rewarding the services of their members without the detriment to the royal patrimony which had hitherto existed. The encomiendas of the orders were, however, permitted to continue in existence.

.   .   .

In accord with the nature of the authority of the immediate lord of the lands concerned, there existed four types of señorío, or dominion, *realengo, abadengo, solariego,* and *behetría*. Dominion of solariego was also known as señorío in a technical sense. These terms apply equally to jurisdiction, the land involved, and the persons under the respective types of jurisdiction. In lands of realengo

---

[7] Subordinate administrative positions with incomes attached in the hierarchy of the Military Orders. (Ed.)

dominion was exclusively of the Crown, in those of solariego dominion was that of lay lords, and in those of abadengo it was that of prelates and churches or monastic foundations and their authorities. Señorío of solariego and abadengo arose from the several types of royal grants and donation. The behetría, the term apparently originating from *benefactoría* or *beneficio,* was a specialized and peculiarly Castilian institution and consisted of a group of subjects who possessed the right to designate their lord. This type of jurisdiction came into existence primarily as a result of the need for protection which existed as a result of the wars with the Moors and the instability to which they gave rise. A group, which frequently included hidalgos, commended themselves to a lord of their choice, himself of necessity a *vecino* of the district concerned, the lord assuming the obligation of protection and the behetrías assuming obligations with respect to tributes and services. The status and rights of the behetrías and the types and amounts of tribute and the types and extent of the services were fixed by fueros issued by the lord after agreement with those who placed themselves under his protection. Individuals also commended themselves in behetría.

There came into existence, as the institution evolved, the *behetría de linage,* or *entre parientes,* and the *behetría de mar á mar.* Communities of behetría de linage were required to select the señor from within a given line, while those of behetría de mar á mar enjoyed the right to choose a lord in any part of the realm and to change *señor* at will.

The lordship of the behetría was hereditary and the holdings were frequently divided among members of the family concerned, each señor being known as a *devisero.* The superior government of the behetría pertained to the lord and the lands of the behetría were composed of his holdings and those of the people of the district. The administration of justice was exercised by the Crown or by the lord, or was divided between the Crown and the lord.

Methods of government differed widely from behetría to behetría. The principal obligation of the vecinos of the behetría was that of the payment of tribute, although limited services were also given. As did methods of government, tribute and service varied greatly. Of the tributes, the Crown and the señor each received stipulated portions.

As Castilian dominion was extended and made permanent, the behetría as an institution lost its value and importance. Since it tended to become a source of dissention among the nobles, Pedro I sought its abolition, but without success. From the latter part of the fourteenth century the behetría degenerated until it became in its final form merely a community of *pecheros* and *labradores*.[8]

Solariegos were those who inhabited the land of a lord and who had descended from the *colonos* and *siervos de la gleba*.[9] They owed obedience to the lord who possessed dominion over the territory which they inhabited and cultivated and gave to him the required services and tributes. These tributes and services were fixed by fueros given by the lords themselves under authority granted by the sovereign, who in certain cases accorded specific confirmation. The land inhabited by the solariegos in the earlier period pertained exclusively to the lord, but later people of this status were permitted a degree of conditioned ownership. The Crown normally retained no prerogatives in such territory except those of the *servitio* and *moneda*.

The personal status of the solariegos was in the Middle Ages in certain respects close to that of serfs in other parts of Europe. In the earlier period the lords possessed extensive powers over the solariegos and they were to some degree bound to the soil. Later, by law and in practice, they were accorded a considerable measure of freedom and were permitted to leave the land on which they lived to establish themselves elsewhere, transferring their allegiance from their original lords to those who held dominion over

---

[8] Taxpayers and farmers. (Ed.)

[9] Types of serfs. (Ed.)

the territories to which they moved. Upon leaving the lands of their original lords and transferring allegiance solariegos forfeited to the former in recompense half of their *solares* and *bienes*. They were permitted to sell the halves of their solares and *bienes inmuebles*[1] not relinquished to the señores and to sell or carry with them half of their movable property. Isabella, in 1480, freed the solariegos from the remaining traces of servile status.

The inhabitants of abadengo owed obedience and gave tributes and services to the spiritual authorities who possessed señorío and to whom the land pertained, bishops, abbots, or other officials of the Church and monastic foundations. As in the case of lands of solariego, the ecclesiastical lords or authorities concerned issued fueros which established the nature and extent of services and tributes, and the prerogatives of the servitio and moneda alone were retained by the Crown. Those of abadengo were frequently known as solariegos de abadengo.

Concejos to carry on, or to participate in, local government existed in towns of behetría and in certain towns of señorío, temporal and ecclesiastical. These concejos were under the superior authority of the lord and the administrative officers appointed by him. People under the dominion of secular and spiritual lords possessed the right to appeal to the Crown concerning oppression and injustices on the part of the señor and his officers, and the sovereign on occasions adopted remedial measures and issued privileges for the benefit and protection of those concerned.

Tributes, imposts, and services were of many types and varied widely. As noted, they were determined with regard to form and extent by the sovereign through laws and fueros and by lay and ecclesiastical lords and the authorities of the military orders by fueros which they themselves issued for their respective holdings under authority of the Crown. Custom, in some cases, also tended to fix the form of certain tributes and services. Tributes and imposts were

---

[1] Immovable property. (Ed.)

given by subjects in kind, wheat, barley, wine, oil, meat, fowls, and eggs being normal types, and in money. These tributes and imposts existed under the designations *infurción, martiniega, marzadga, censos, fumazga, pechos, fonsadera, montadgo, diezmos, anubda, conducho, yantar, posadas, devisa, mincio, naturaleza,* and other terms. With respect to actual practice it is difficult, if not impossible, to distinguish between certain of these tributes: some of the designating terms are of both general and specific connotations, and others may be, in instances, synonymous.

The infurción was of general application and was given in recognition of direct dominion, and the fonsadera was owed to the Crown alone. Tributes were given on days and upon occasions designated by law or fuero. Navidad, the Día de San Juan, and the Día de San Martín were among the days commonly designated. The martiniega took its name from the Día de San Martín and the marzadga from the month of March. The yantar consisted in the supplying of foodstuffs to the king or lord when he visited the city or town and the conducho in the furnishing of lodging, clothing, and forage. In its aspects with regard to tribute, the fonsadera was paid to support expenses for the conduct of war and in commutation of personal military service.

Personal service was of various types. The most important of these services were agricultural labor in all of its aspects, labor on the public works undertaken by the Crown, lord, or local government and other types of labor imposed by the Crown or lord. These services were known as the *facendera,* or *serna.* It was the obligation of the señor, at least in some cases, to provide sustenance for those engaged in such labor during the periods of service. The fonsadera in its aspects with respect to service consisted in the duty of contributing personally to the works on walls and fortresses. The term fosadera may be synonymous with fonsadera in its connotations in connection with actual service. Other specific services were the clearing of land, included in the facendera, or serna, the cutting and carrying of wood for the lord, and mounting guard at the castle and at the gates of the town. The times at which these services were to be rendered and the periods of duration were fixed by fuero and custom. Military service, the *fonsado,* was required.

Mudéjares[2] and Jews in the realms of Castile were, until their forced conversion or expulsion, under the protection (*commanda, specialis guardia*) of the king, to whom their persons belonged. The sovereign could not, however, consign them to personal service. Their patrimonies pertained to the Crown, and only with the permission of the king could they alienate bienes inmuebles. They had the right to move about freely. Castilian law required that specific *cartas de gracia* be given periodically by the Crown to define and fix the status of the Mudéjares under the protection of the sovereign, while Jews as a group were under permanent protection. In the cases of some smaller towns of Mudéjares these were granted exclusive possession by the Crown, Christians being forbidden to enter such places. A considerable number of Mudéjares, through grants of territory and towns, were under the dominion of nobles, the Church, and the military orders.

With the exception of Mudéjares under the authority of the nobles, the Church, and the military orders, the Crown determined the status of the Mudéjares and Jews in all of its aspects and fixed the taxes which they were required to pay. By agreement or royal dispensation the Jews and Mudéjares were permitted to practice their respective religions, and the latter were permitted to retain their own law.

Mudéjares and Jews residing in the Castilian cities and towns were set apart from the remainder of the population in special districts, known as *aljamas* and *arrabales.* Moorish and Jewish authorities exercised civil and criminal jurisdiction over their own people, subject to the superior authority of the Crown, a body of four or five *adelantados* presiding over the Jewish communities and individual

---

[2] Muslims living under Christian rule. (Ed.)

cadíes (*kadís*) exercising authority over the Moorish. Nobles, prelates, and the officials of the military orders who held Mudéjares in dominion determined their status and fixed tributes and services by fueros which they issued.

The origins of the repartimiento-encomienda of the Indies are to be sought not in any one of the Castilian grants, donations, institutions, and forms which have been discussed, but in these latter as a whole. The Crown, conquistadors, royal officers, and colonists placed in operation in the New World practices which had existed in Castile over a long period and which were an established part of the structure of society in that kingdom, and fused, adapted, and transformed them to meet the special conditions and circumstances which were encountered there. This process resulted in the evolution of a new institution, an institution which rested upon the general complex of Castilian grants and donations and the pattern of institutions, usages, and practices which were organically connected with them, and one which assumed a place among the mercedes which the sovereigns of Castile accorded to their vassals in reward of services and in furtherance of their policies.

Certain broader analogies between the repartimiento-encomienda and the grants, donations, and institutions of Castile are relatively clear. All existed for the same general purposes and were directed toward the same objectives with respect to the rewarding of services, the establishment of the obligation of continued service, and the provision of military defense. Analogy between the New World institution and certain Castilian forms also exists with relation to the objectives of the peopling and permanent holding of territory acquired by conquest.

Since the repartimiento-encomienda was exclusively a royal grant and was invariably assigned by governmental officers directly in the name of the sovereign, the closest parallels are to be found, on a purely juridical basis, in the grants of Castile which were conceded by the Crown. This does not signify, however, that analogies do not exist in Castilian donations granted by other overlords, both temporal and ecclesiastical, as the general forms of such donations were in the broader sense identical with those made by the Crown and the practices connected with them were basically the same.

The fundamental and essential juridical difference between the Castilian grants and donations and the repartimiento-encomienda in its final form is to be found in jurisdiction. The former carried governmental powers and jurisdiction in varying degrees, delegated by the Crown or other overlord, while the latter did not. In Castile, the inhabitants of the territory over which a lord held dominion were the vassals of the latter as well as of the sovereign: in the Indies the natives were the free and direct vassals of the Crown alone. However, the assumption of jurisdiction by the encomenderos during the early period indicates a definite extra-legal application of Castilian practice on a basis of señorío in the technical sense. It is to be noted that in assuming jurisdiction the encomenderos acted in all things as the representatives of the sovereign, and in his name. After the exercise of jurisdiction had been terminated by Crown legislation and general administrative forms had been formalized, the government of the Indian towns was carried on exclusively by officers of the royal government and by local native officials and cabildos. In these cabildos and native officers of the Indian towns is to be found a parallel to the concejos of towns held by Castilian lords, although it is to be recalled that these latter were under the control of the señor and the officials appointed by him, and an analogy to the government of the aljamas and towns of Mudéjares and Jewish districts by their own representatives under the superior authority of Crown officials.

The basic elements of service and tribute existed in the institutions of Castile and in the repartimiento-encomienda in its earlier form, and tribute remained a basic element throughout the existence of the American institution. The forms of service and tribute, if only through the sheer force of the circumstances which universally governed such institutions, were of the same essential nature in Castile and in the Indies, being imposed in accord with the agricultural and mineral resources of the areas concerned and the activities of the people. The establishment of the obligations that the natives render tributes and services to the encomenderos and the authorization of these practices by the Crown placed in effect Castilian usage which was of long standing in connection with the relationship between lords and their peoples. The imposition of tributes and services by the encomenderos at their will before the elimination of services and establishment of official *tasaciones* parallels the granting of fueros stipulating the forms and extent of tributes by lords in Castile. However, at no time during the early period did the encomenderos stipulate the tributes and services to be given through formal documents which might roughly correspond to the fueros given by lords in Castile. The encomenderos, under law, provided for the sustenance of the natives while they were engaged in services in the same manner as did the lords of Castile in instances provide sustenance for their subjects when they were performing service. Upon the formalization of the repartimiento-encomienda the direct representatives of the Crown fixed tributes in accord with general royal ordinances, these tributes being indicated in official documents. Between this practice and the establishment of tributes and services by the Crown in Castilian lands of realengo through specific fueros there exists a rough parallel. The methods of giving tributes in the Indies were based on those of Castile, and after the regularization of the encomienda payment was made at fixed periods and at specific times, as was payment in Castile. It is to be noted that the Día de San Juan and Navidad were among the times that tribute was to be given both in Castile and in the Indies.

As has already been suggested, the greater and lesser

conquistadors and *pobladores*[3] with the support of governmental officials, sought, as encomenderos, to achieve for themselves the dominion and status of the *señores de vasallos*[4] of Castile, with grants in perpetuity, jurisdiction, and land ownership, and their acts and policies toward the natives in the period before the establishment of close royal control were in consonance with this determination. In tending to regard the natives assigned to them as their vassals and in assuming jurisdictional powers the encomenderos in the period prior to the regularization of the encomienda arrogated to themselves the authority and prerogatives of Castilian señores de vasallos, and señorío in the technical sense was the type of dominion which, frequently with the support of greater and lesser officials of the royal government, they legally sought to attain for themselves at the hands of the Crown, both before and after the formalization of the institution. Through appointing major-domos and other agents to aid them in the administration of their encomiendas in the early period the encomenderos further placed in effect the practices of Castilian lords. Moreover, the tendency on the part of the encomenderos to consider the districts assigned to them as their property and their appropriation of lands within these districts indicate that they regarded the status of the lands concerned as approximating that of territory assigned in repartimiento in Castile by juro de heredad. The repartimiento in Castile, it is to be pointed out, was primarily a partition of lands, although vassals were frequently included, and this fact was undoubtedly in the minds of the early encomenderos. The transfer and sale of encomiendas by encomenderos in the early period also indicates a tendency to regard grants in repartimiento-encomienda as being by juro de heredad.

The legal status which was actually accorded to the

---

[3] Settlers. (Ed.)

[4] Lords of serfs. (Ed.)

encomenderos by the Crown would appear to be an adaptation and attenuation of the types of dominion inherent in the Castilian encomienda, feudo, tierra, and tenencia. Grants of the encomienda were definitely of limited duration and were transmitted in succession under definite laws only for the number of lives specified by the Crown. The number of lives was frequently extended by the sovereign, and in this practice a certain analogy is found with that connected with those of the Castilian grants which were given for lifetime and extended by the Crown or other lord to a second generation upon the death of the original recipient. With regard to tenure there is also a certain parallel between the encomienda and the feudo, which was hereditary to and including the grandson of the original grantee. In its final form the encomienda was in many respects closely analogous to the Castilian *tierra,* a royal grant of revenues from stipulated towns or districts. It should be noted, however, that grants in tierra at times carried jurisdiction, which the encomienda did not. Land ownership was never made a feature of the encomienda of the Indies, and usufruct was the only right with respect to the land which was accorded to the encomenderos by the Crown.

Commendation was one of the most essential of the principles which underlay the institution of the encomienda. In this it was comparable to the earlier and later forms of the Castilian encomienda, the prestimonio, the mandación, the feudo, and the encomienda of the military orders. Under all of these latter titles persons were placed under the protection and guardianship of señores by the Crown and other overlords, while with the repartimiento-encomienda of the Indies the sovereign through his representatives placed natives in the charge of the encomenderos to advance their well-being and assure their Christianization. The people concerned were in all of these instances commended to the care of others by a higher agency. It should be pointed out in this connection that those under dominion of behetría commended themselves to their señores, as did those in the early days of the Reconquista who placed themselves, for whatever cause, under the protection of lords.

With respect to the donations and grants of Castile, it was understood that the lord was obligated to protect the people under his dominion, whatever might be the type of señorío he possessed. In connection with certain types of holdings this obligation was, moreover, definitely asserted. The Crown specifically established the obligation that the encomendero of the New World protect and aid the natives granted to him in encomienda and this requirement was included in the *cédulas* of encomienda.

The repartimiento of conquered lands among the conquistadors by the sovereigns of Castile in reward of services has a direct application with regard to the evolution of the repartimiento-encomienda in the Indies. The practice of the repartimiento, originating in the early days of the Reconquista and continuing through the final conquest of the kingdom of Granada, afforded a usage which, with adaptation, was readily applicable in the Indies. As already indicated, the repartimiento of Castile connoted basically a division of lands, but also in instances included vassals. The transition from a partition of territory in Castile to the partition of natives on a territorial basis in the Indies was a natural one. The fact that the partitions of Castile at times included people is, moreover, of significance, as in such assignments of subjects is found precedent of long standing for the division and granting of Indians. The requirement of residence connected with the repartimiento of Castile was paralleled by that established for the encomenderos of the Indies. The partition and assignment of lands in repartimiento in Castile was carried out directly by the sovereign or by authorities designated by him. In the Indies the repartimiento and assignment of natives was made in the name of the sovereign by his representatives. Officials of Castile who were delegated powers to carry out the repartimiento were known as repartidores, and officials of the Indies who conducted partitions took the same title.

The Crown established the obligation that the encomendero further the Christianization of the natives assigned to him as an essential feature of the encomienda. Thus a religious element was introduced into the institution. Encomiendas of the military orders entailed the obligation on the part of the comendadores that they give alms to the needy, support the curas of their encomiendas and repair and maintain the churches of their holdings. This type of grant consequently included certain religious requirements. Between the obligation of the comendadores of the military orders to support curas and repair and maintain the churches of their encomiendas and the requirement that the encomenderos of the Indies construct and maintain churches or chapels and support curas or chaplains in their towns, or otherwise aid the *doctrina,* there would appear to be a direct analogy. The religious obligations of the comendadores of the military orders may have served as a precedent for and a basis of the more extensive religious obligations established by the Crown as essential features of the repartimiento-encomienda. It must be emphasized, however, that the advancement of the spiritual and material welfare of the Indians and their christianization and entrance within the fold of the Church was from the first the "principal intent" of the Crown and that consequently the sovereigns would undoubtedly have established religious obligations as an essential feature of the repartimiento-encomienda regardless of practice in Castile. Furthermore, it is to be assumed that religious ministration to the people of their holdings was an essential part of the obligations of prelates and abbots who held dominion.

In connection with the early development of the repartimiento-encomienda in the West Indian islands, it should be noted that Francisco de Bobadilla and Nicolás de Ovando[5] were both comendadores of military orders and that through the possession of high office in Española they were

---

[5] Bobadilla, governor of Hispaniola, 1500–1502; Ovando, governor, 1502–1509. (Ed.)

in a position to exercise great influence on the institution in the earliest stages of its evolution. The latter, acting on the basis of royal ordinances and through his own initiative in the exercise of authority as governor, introduced forms which decisively influenced the development of the original repartimiento into the repartimiento-encomienda through establishing in a practical sense the requirement that the recipients of grants of natives assume obligations with respect to furthering the welfare of the latter and assuring their Christianization. The term encomienda, furthermore, appears to have made its appearance in the Indies coincident with the forms introduced by Ovando, that of repartimiento having hitherto been applied to the grants of natives to the colonists of Española.

The extent to which Ovando was influenced by knowledge of the actual operations of the encomiendas of the military orders and the degree to which he may have consciously placed in effect practices and obligations connected with that type of grant in building on the original repartimiento in Española is an interesting and important point of speculation.

The obligation that the encomenderos render military service as a condition of tenure finds its direct counterpart in the service required of recipients of all types of Castilian grants and donations, and the requirement that the former maintain arms and a horse is analogous to that which obliged the latter to support a stipulated number of men-at-arms or to possess a horse and arms. The oath of fealty to the sovereign sworn by the encomenderos is a parallel of the ceremony of pleito-homenaje related with Castilian grants, and the ceremony by which the encomenderos were placed in "possession" of their towns and Indians is roughly analogous to that of investiture. Furthermore, the forms and wording of the New World cédulas of encomienda were in many respects similar to those of the titles and diplomas by which the grants and donations of Castile were conceded.

The people of lands of realengo were subject to military

service for the sovereign, and those of solariego and abadengo were required to give such service to the Crown and to their lords. They were required, also, to give tributes to meet the expenses of war. In this connection it should be pointed out that certain of the greater conquistadors, as royal officers, secured native auxiliaries and burden bearers from the towns they held in encomienda and that they levied tributes in these towns specifically for the purpose of meeting the costs of expeditions of discovery and conquest.

The personal status of the Indians assigned in encomienda under law as free and direct vassals of the Crown and persons who were under the guardianship of the sovereign is comparable to that of Castilian subjects under several types of dominion. The status of the natives in its several aspects may be compared with that of the people of lands of realengo, that of solariegos after their liberation from servile status, that of the inhabitants of behetrías which degenerated into communities of pecheros and labradores, and that of the Mudéjares and Jews, who until their forced conversion or expulsion were under the special protection of the Crown. To attempt to establish analogies with regard to status which are completely valid on a legal basis, however, is extremely difficult. The establishment of the legal position of the Indians, it is to be recalled, was attended by prolonged and complicated deliberation on the part of the Crown. Nevertheless, it is possible to indicate certain broader parallels and contrasts. The inhabitants of lands of salariego (señorío), abadengo, and behetría, and those of the encomiendas of the military orders, as their subjects, rendered tributes and services to the señores. In the same manner the Indians at first gave services and tributes, and later tributes alone, to their encomenderos. The tributes and services of the former were fixed by the lords through fueros, while those of the natives of the Indies were established by the encomenderos in the early period, and thereafter by direct agencies of the royal government. People of lands of realengo were the direct vassals of the Crown alone, as were the Indians, and gave tribute and service only to the sovereign. Mudéjares and Jews were under special guardianship of the sovereign, as were the Indians. Both Mudéjares and Jews of aljamas were governed by their own representatives under supervision of royal officers: the native towns were governed by Indian officials and cabildos supervised by Castilian officials. Before their forced conversion, Mudéjares and Jews were permitted to retain their own religions, and the Mudéjares were permitted to retain their law. The natives of the New World were from the first required to accept Christianity and enter within the Church, and they were subject to Castilian law. Mudéjares under the dominion of lords were subjected to tributes and services in the same manner and by the same forms as were Castilians who were under the dominion of señores. Those of Castile under the dominion of lords possessed the right to appeal to the Crown for redress of grievances at the hands of their lords: the Indians had the right to appeal to agencies and officials of the royal government concerning mistreatment, abuses, and infractions of law on the part of the encomenderos.

While it is not possible to reach definite conclusions at the present time, it may be suggested that the types of dominion, institutions, forms and practices from which the repartimiento-encomienda in its ultimate form evolved more directly than from others were the tierra, the encomienda granted by the Crown and other overlords, the encomienda of the military orders, the repartimiento, and the usages connected with lands of realengo and their inhabitants. From all of these proceeded definite elements which, through the interaction of Crown policy and the acts and practices of officials of the Indies and the encomenderos, and in accord with circumstances and expediency, were fused and adapted to bring the American institution into being.

7

JOHN PRESTON MOORE

THE URBAN HERITAGE

*Although the Castilian Crown consistently opposed
the proliferation of encomiendas in the New World, it
looked with somewhat more indulgent eyes upon the
establishment of towns. The latter, as John Preston
Moore shows in this selection, had been brought
increasingly under royal control since the early fourteenth century, when Alfonso XI first appointed royal
corregidores to supervise their affairs. In spite of ever
increasing royal pressure, the relative leniency toward
towns permitted them to preserve, at least for a time,
some of the traditions of elective government that
began in Iberia with the establishment of the first
chartered towns behind the frontier in the tenth century.*

*Professor Moore took his doctorate at Northwest-
ern University in 1936 and is now Professor of
History at Louisiana State University. He was a
Guggenheim Fellow in 1960–1961 and has specialized
in the history of eighteenth-century Ecuador and
Peru. Aside from articles in scholarly journals and the*

From John Preston Moore, *The Cabildo in Peru Under the
Hapsburgs* (Durham, N.C.: Duke University Press, 1954),
pp. 15–28. Reprinted by permission of Duke University Press.

*book from which the present selection is taken, he has
also written* The Cabildo in Peru Under the Bourbons,
1700–1824.

A *vecino*[1] of the Castilian town of the thirteenth century
had an exceptionally favorable all-around status compared
to his fellow living in sixteenth-century Spain and America.
Properly speaking, the term signified all heads of families
and landowners, whether having residence behind the solid
walls and ramparts or in the open country. In order to
obtain this position one had to establish a domicile in the
limits of the city, which in Seville was fixed at twelve years
to discourage migratory tendencies so prevalent in the
Middle Ages, to have his name inscribed on the official roll
of citizenry, and to be willing to fulfill the obligations
recorded in the *fuero*.[2] For the retention of this status he
must provide a substitute to perform his civic duties if he
were absent from the town for a considerable period of
time. Indefinite or prolonged absence resulted in forfeiture
of citizenship. From the viewpoint of the rise of representative government citizenship carried with it the significant privilege of taking part in the election of town
officials. It was a paramount right, the exercise of which
was jealously guarded. There were other privileges touch-
ing the administration of justice and providing occasional
exemption from royal financial impositions. When accused
of a misdemeanor, he might stand trial in his own court,
namely that of the alcalde, where he would receive justice
according to municipal law. Some prominent individuals,
securing from the king the title of *caballero,* were relieved
from payment of the tribute. No one was excused, however, from the obligation of bearing arms when the city

---

[1] Citizen households, literally, "neighbor." (Ed.)

[2] Town charter, usually granted by the king or another lord.
(Ed.)

was threatened or when it was deemed necessary to dispatch a contingent to the royal or seignorial force by virtue of the terms of the charter.

A more numerous section of the population were classified as *moradores,* or lodgers. In contrast to the *vecinos,* members of this group did not maintain as a rule separate households, instead renting rooms or quarters. Nor were they landowners. Thus merchants with living arrangements in the rear of their shops and establishments belonged to this category of municipal resident. The principal handicap to the *morador* was exclusion from participation in the deliberations of the *concejo.* There was little distinction between the two types of municipal dwellers in the payment of taxes and duties and in the performance of military service. A somewhat similar cleavage is to be observed among the residents of the colonial town.

With the augmenting of the population of the municipality because of improved conditions of law and order and the expansion of trade, the *concejo,* of Germanic origin, found itself superseded at the beginning of the thirteenth century as a governmental unit by a small group of officeholders. Its fundamental defect was that it was too cumbersome and unwieldy for the proper conduct of the town's affairs. The assumption of its powers by the local magistracy was an inevitable outcome. In some places the democratic governing assembly, realizing its inadequacy in dealing with the complexities of civic administration, voluntarily yielded its authority. While the *concejo's* influence was steadily reduced, resulting in advantage and profit for the body of magistrates and councilors, it continued to meet occasionally as an open assembly for the discussion of questions of great moment before the town. In the final development of this trend the municipal council formed a closed corporation known by a variety of names, the *cabildo, justicia, regimiento,* and *ayuntamiento.* The number of those comprising the *ayuntamiento* in the thirteenth century differed according to the size and prestige of the municipality. Its chief functionaries were ordinarily the alcaldes *ordinarios,* usually two or more individuals, elected for one year and having administrative duties and primary jurisdiction in civil and criminal cases, and the *regidores,* or aldermen, with authority in general conciliar business. For example, Burgos, one of the most important municipalities, had a council of sixteen members, excluding the alcaldes and a royal judge.

The list of lesser officials in the thirteenth century was extensive and varied. In Seville there were the *jurados,* who were entrusted with drawing up the roll of citizens and, in addition, who performed military duties; *fieles,* who rendered decisions in cases of an economic nature; *almotacenes,* or clerks of the market, charged with oversight of the exchange so as to preclude the fixing of excessive prices and the selling of articles and goods unable to meet the standards of quality or size and weight; *alamines,* or assistants to the *almotacenes; mayordomos,* responsible for the handling of the municipal *propios,* or properties, and the disbursal of civic funds; *procuradores,* serving in a dual capacity as representatives of the municipality at the Cortes and as attorneys to plead civic cases before royal and seignorial courts; *alguacil mayor,* head of law enforcement in the district; *alférez,* or commander of the civic militia; *alarifes,* or inspectors of public works; *veladores,* or watchmen; *andadores* and *mensajeros,* or council messengers. Few if any of these officials were paid by the *cabildo,* the concept of the salaried functionary being essentially a modern development. Instead, they secured remuneration through the perquisites of their offices, charging for services rendered and pocketing the fines levied for the infraction of regulations. It will be noted that a great percentage of these offices appeared in the colonial municipality, with, however, some changes in their attributes, and that the notion of office as a form of property likewise prevailed in the new regions.

Social and racial stratification played a role in the determination of municipal affairs. As a rule the dominant element was the rising middle class drawn from property owners, merchants, traders, members of the professions and well-to-do artisans. In nearly all of the cities there existed an aristocracy of the *caballeros,* having its origin in the performance of military services. The title of *caballero* was usually granted by the king to a limited number of loyal subjects whose resources enabled them to possess a horse and arms. Sevilla had two grades of this aristocracy, those named by Alfonso the Wise in granting of the *fuero* of Toledo, and those subsequently conceded the title *de merced.* The urban nobility held membership in some councils, while in other cities it was customary for plebeians to fill the important offices. There were towns where representation was equally divided between nobles and commoners. The population of the city often contained special racial or national groups having a minor and negligible say in conciliar affairs. In Andalusia Moorish elements persisted as physicians, landowners, and artisans. Not infrequently there was a ghetto, which though within the walled confines, was apparently not a part of the *concejo's* jurisdiction. As a maritime city Seville had aggregates of foreign nationalities, of Genoese and French, and a special section, inhabited by *gente de mar,* or seafaring folk, with unique rights and concessions from the king.

In the administration of justice in the thirteenth century the power of the alcalde, assisted by the councils, was at first fairly extensive. Municipalities in the royal territory were allowed much control over judicial functions with right of appeal to the king's courts in serious civil and criminal cases. Monarchical authority in this sphere was represented by *merinos* and *adelantados,* appointed by the crown as regional administrators. During the later Middle Ages conditions arose within the municipalities leading to the enlargement of royal jurisdiction at the expense of the alcaldes. Notorious abuses were committed by the *alguaciles* and other local officers; and in many places there were a growing disregard for law and a tendency toward class warfare caused in large part by a monopoly of conciliar posts by the urban aristocracy. To check this deplorable trend and at the same time to increase its own power the crown expanded the scope of its jurisdiction. The royal judges had special cognizance in the execution of the criminal code, settling all cases involving death by violence, altercation on the highway, rape, and the desecration of sanctified areas. Moreover, civil suits arising between municipalities and between a municipality and a nobleman were to be adjudicated in the king's court.

The *fuero* conceded to the town the right to a *hacienda*, or treasury. Its principal revenue was derived from property acquired during the Reconquest to which title was recognized in the charter. Land attached to the municipality was inalienable and of two main types: municipal and communal. "The first-mentioned, called *propios* or *bienes concejiles*, were the cultivated or agricultural lands. They were administered by the town officials and either worked in common, by rotation, or rented. In any case the proceeds were applied to the support of the local government and to pay taxes to higher authorities. The communal lands, properly speaking (*bienes comunales*), consisted of woodland, pastures, and a separate, well-defined area usually located just outside the city gates known as the *ejido*." For the wealthier communes *propios* also included ovens, brickkilns, warehouses, taverns, and slaughterhouses, leased to the highest bidder annually or for a number of years. Private property existed alongside the municipally owned lands in the form of town lots, or *solares*, cultivated strips in the surrounding area, or *heredades*, and other holdings. A second source of income came from taxes, the collection of which was leased to individuals or associations. They included excises on certain commodities of common consumption, such as meat, bread, and wine, duties on circulation of goods, fees for the use of standards of weight and measure, and an array of special impositions, some of which originally belonged to the crown, but which had been granted as a favor to the municipality. When the treasury found itself hard pressed for funds to meet the outlay for defense or a request from the crown, an extraordinary assessment from the well-to-do *vecinos* was in order. *Mayordomos,* paying out funds upon authorization of the cabildo, turned their accounts over to *contadores,* who, after checking, furnished necessary receipts. Another source of municipal income was fines imposed by local officers for the violation of ordinances. From certain customary royal taxes or levies the charter sometimes gave complete or partial exemption in line with the crown's policy of favoring municipal growth. But for the most part the sum owed by the town in lieu of military service continued to be collected, and the right of hospitality due the monarch on his travels throughout the realm prevailed.

Town officials wielded some authority over two species of communal organizations prominent in the Middle Ages: the guilds and the *confradías,* or confraternities. The earliest business association was the merchant guild, composed of the principal merchants of the locality. A second organization embraced all individuals engaged in the same trade or type of economic activity, such as the butchers and bakers, called the craft guilds. Both institutions enjoyed influence and prestige and served to satisfy not only the economic but the social needs of their members. The confraternities, on the other hand, were primarily religious associations, designed to fulfill some specific social objective, the giving of a dinner in honor of a deceased person of distinction, or the performance of a charitable act. The guilds and the sodalities alike had an element of mutual assistance for their participants.

No communal privilege had greater potentiality for shaping the future course of central government than that of representation in the national assembly, or the Cortes. While some kind of unsystematic, occasional representation existed in the Cortes of León and Castile in the latter part of the twelfth century, it is more than likely that no regular, organized scheme of corporate action, "in which agents responsible to their constituents, even though they must obey a superior jurisdiction in the king's court and council," developed before the second half of the thirteenth century. It was only after the municipalities had secured charters that the king recognized their importance by issuing to a limited number of them an invitation to join the nobles and the clergy in the *curia*. In summoning the municipal procurators the king was moved primarily by a need for funds for the expenses of his government and palace and for the prosecution of foreign wars and the subduing of the rebellious nobility. Less significant was his desire to seek the advice and counsel of the burghers. Hence during the early period of the Cortes' existence the municipalities attended reluctantly and because of compulsion. The reverse is true in a subsequent era when the Cortes had acquired legislative rights. Each town invited by the crown to the *curia* customarily dispatched two procurators, although it was not until the Cortes of Madrid, 1429–1430, that the number was set specifically at this figure. The delegates were selected by diverse methods, by balloting in the *cabildo,* by drawing lots, by rotation, or by a combination of these devices.

At the beginning of the fourteenth century the representatives of the Third Estate in Castile possessed considerable power. It was more extensive than that enjoyed by the English burghers of the same era. In both England and Spain the source of this authority was financial. Whenever the monarch required any sum beyond the usual contributions or taxes from the municipalities, it was expected that he would obtain the assembly's consent for the appropriation. Through the approval of extraordinary taxes the Cortes, like Parliament in the British Isles, had a powerful weapon for the redress of grievances. While there was no constitutional obligation upon the king to accede to these remonstrances, it was soon discovered that concessions paved the way for financial grants. Having secured monetary authority, the national assembly developed legislative prerogatives. Without consulting the king, it drew up petitions of both a general and specific nature, which, it was expected, would be enacted into law. Some of them dealt with the reduction of taxes, a definition of the authority of royal agents, and the curbing of banditry. The assemblies of 1339 (Madrid), 1348 (Alcalá), 1351 (Valladolid), 1366 (Burgos), 1371 (Toro), 1373 (Toro), 1377 (Burgos), and 1380 (Soria) promulgated a large number of such ordinances, evidence of a zealous preoccupation with the affairs of the kingdom. When these ordinances had received royal sanction, they became essentially a part of the law of the land.

Finally, within the framework of the charter, the Castilian town of the thirteenth century was permitted to take measures for the maintenance of civic order and peace and for the defense against external enemies. Local officers were charged with the suppression of the all-too-frequent riots and disturbances, the bane of existence for the medieval urban dweller. To protect the inhabitants from attacks by the Moors, by lawless nobles, and by rival cities, the town authorities constructed around the populated area high, massive walls with barbicans at regular intervals. Castles, manned by civic forces, were erected in the district for further defense. *Vecinos, moradores,* and residents of the small outlying settlements and villages governed by the city owed military duty. A contingent of townsmen, whose numbers and duration of service were fixed by the *fuero,* might be summoned by the king to join the royal host.

As a supplementary military measure, towns banded together in the twelfth century in leagues known as *hermandades.* It is likely that they originated to a greater extent from the impotence of the monarchy than from the need for further defense from the Moors. They were directed mainly against the nobility, but under exceptional circumstances against the king, if he threatened municipal liberties. The government of the league centered in an assembly of delegates from the municipalities meeting to deliberate on common policy. In general the associations were temporary in nature and were dissolved as soon as the immediate objective had been reached.

Because of the weakness of the crown, due chiefly to the

unremitting struggle with the nobles, the Castilian cities retained a generous degree of political and administrative freedom almost to the middle of the fourteenth century. Such was this freedom that some places handled questions of foreign relations and diplomacy through their leagues and engaged at will in wars with the Moors, with the aristocracy, and with civic rivals. The king was often powerless to quell the outbreak of fighting, with the result that in some regions a virtual state of anarchy reigned. During this period many seignorial and ecclesiastical cities struggled to vindicate their rights against their overlords and established themselves in a more enviable status. Despite these gains, the Castilian municipalities never attained the state of liberty held by the Flemish and Italian cities, largely because the circumstances of the Reconquest required a greater exercise of authority by the crown.

But this condition of comparative freedom, reaching its apogee in the thirteenth century, was not destined to permanency. By the first half of the following century signs of decay and disintegration were apparent. Turmoil and disorder, arising from factional jealousies and rivalries, developed in the municipalities. Commoners were pitted against aristocrats, who looked to the crown to uphold their rights. Feeling themselves discriminated against by the great cities to which they were subject, many small towns asserted their independence and secured charters from the king, recognizing him as their overlord. In some cities prolonged domestic strife caused the middle class to appeal directly to the monarch for intervention and the restoration of law and order, vital for the conduct of trade and the continuance of their prosperity. In the municipal administrative system several unsavory features began to make their appearance: venality of officeholders, invention of superfluous posts, and multiple tenure of office. Some of the cities avoided these defects and troubled conditions and so preserved their liberties until the latter part of the fifteenth century.

Municipal decline was hastened by the adoption of a

different policy on the part of the crown. During the critical period of the monarch's struggle with the ambitious but lawless nobles the Castilian cities had rendered indispensable aid in money and men and had secured in return extensive political and economic rights. By the first quarter of the fourteenth century the king, influenced by the revival of Roman legal theories and temporarily supreme over feudal resistance, saw his way clear to proceed toward the attainment of the ultimate ideal of absolutism. The Castilian cities were blind to the golden opportunity, realized in England, of joining with the lesser nobility to strengthen the Cortes as a permanent check on the development of royal authority. The resurgence of feudal power in the first half of the fifteenth century again pointed up the necessity of cooperation between the nobles and the Third Estate.

Alfonso XI, reigning in Castile from 1325–1350, was the first to follow a consistent policy directed at weakening the power of the urban governments. Maladministration and instability on the local level furnished both a pretext and a cause for royal interference. It was his aim to undermine rather than to abrogate the *fueros*. At his instigation the Cortes of Alcalá (1348) named *corregidores*, or royal agents, who could be dispatched at the invitation of the citizenry to towns needing advice and aid. The crown abused its privilege by sending these officials whenever it saw fit without considering the wishes of the local councils. Serving with the *regidores* and the alcaldes, they illegally assumed authority to the king's profit. Alfonso XI increased royal prestige by initiating the system of royal *regidores* when he designated in 1343 to the council of Segovia a certain number of his retainers, who were to function alongside the regularly elected aldermen. In Seville he nominated twenty-four from the class of loyal *caballeros* to act as *regidores*. Through the efforts of these representatives many local ordinances affirming freedom were altered or withdrawn altogether. With the introduction of the sale of offices under John II, 1406–1454, conciliar elections began to disappear.

In vain did the municipalities protest to the king against the loss of their privileges. They petitioned that the *corregidor's* tenure of office be limited to one year and that the individual chosen for the office be a resident of the community in which he was to serve. In the Cortes there were affirmations by procurators of the right of the towns to decide whether or not royal agents should be sent to them. During John II's reign municipal delegates memorialized the ruler to the end that "the *corregidores*, at the expiration of their term, be obliged to remain for at least fifty days in the region where they had held office, so that any one who believed himself to have been wronged by their verdicts might state his case and have justice." Although the king did not grant this request immediately, the procedure was subsequently adopted and became a regular governmental institution. Called the *residencia*, or residence, it was in essence a judicial investigation by the crown of officials at the expiry of their term of office. So effective was the practice in Castile that it was carried over to America during the establishment of the colonies as a means of checking the rapacity and injustice of the royal agents and likewise of insuring the supremacy of the crown.

Under the Catholic Kings, Ferdinand of Aragon and Isabella of Castile, authority over the cities was augmented. Toward local government the keynote of their policy was centralization and improvement of administration through intervention. Despite earlier measures of reform, corruption and mismanagement existed on a wide scale. The evils of factionalism, with its resultant disorders, caused Isabella to take steps toward its elimination in Cáceres. After a personal visit to the city in 1477 the Queen abolished the annual election of magistrates, thereafter to be selected by lot for life tenure, and in the event of decease of these officials, the vacancies to be filled by the crown. This action was seemingly not displeasing to the people, "because it put a stop to their quarrels and the evils that followed in their train, which had resulted from the elections of earlier days." A wholesale attack on municipal liberties came in the ordinances passed by the Cortes of Toledo in 1480, which further circumscribed local control over conciliar offices. The crown was authorized to cancel hereditary offices and to prevent transfer of positions to relatives and friends. Leasing of the office of *regidor* was forbidden and violations were punishable by forfeiture. In order to dignify the transacting of municipal business it was enjoined that cities without town halls should proceed to erect suitable buildings for this purpose within a stated period. Copies of ordinances and rights should be carefully preserved in the municipal archives. While the tenor of this legislation curtailed local liberties, its beneficial results mitigated some of the civic resentment that it might otherwise have provoked.

These measures contributed no little to the absolutist goal which the Catholic Rulers had in sight. Yet Isabella relied more heavily on another instrumentality, that of enhancing the power and prestige of royal agents in the towns. *Pesquisidores,* having the right of inquiry into the functioning of municipal law and of deciding important cases beyond the scope of the magistrate's ability, and *veedores,* with the duty of overseeing the conduct of public officials and in particular of checking the accounts of the municipal treasurers, were regularly dispatched to the cities and towns. Of far more utility to the crown in the realization of its ambition than these officials were the *corregidores.* After 1480 no city in Castile was free of their presence. A pragmatica, issued at Seville in 1500, minutely defined their duties and responsibilities. After taking the oath of office from the Council of Castile, they were forbidden to associate themselves with local interests either by buying lots or land within the districts to which they were assigned or by selecting their assistants from people of the community. Their instructions called for a close supervision and inspection of municipal affairs. Thus they were to make sure that the municipalities did not erect new castles and positions of defense threatening the central government. Local ordinances might be amended in conjunction with the *regidores*. Taxation must be constantly kept in view so that no new imposts could be levied, and local sources of income, especially that derived from public lands, should be scrutinized with the hope of finding better ways of utilizing the properties. Within the purview of the office came direction of the administration of justice in the field of civil and criminal law, control of the police, prevention of disputes between Moors and Christians—in short, general responsibility for the functioning of local government under the outstretched arms of the crown. To insure the careful selection of these officials and an honest performance of duties, the Catholic Rulers perfected the machinery of the *residencia*. Every *corregidor* at the end of his term of office must submit to the judicial examination and inquiry, to last for thirty days instead of fifty as formerly. The *pesquisidor,* who had in the past presided over this court, was now replaced by a *juez de residencia,* provided with detailed orders. Notice of the forthcoming residence should be announced everywhere throughout the district and in ample time so that any persons having grievances against the *corregidor* would be able to present their cases to the judge. Moreover, the *juez de residencia* was instructed to make every effort to get at the truth of the complaints in order that justice might be done. Through the extension of the office of *corregidor* to all parts of Castile and the universal application of the inquiry, the avowed aim of the Catholic Kings came a step nearer being materialized.

In harmony with their great objective of centralizing the government of the realm, Ferdinand and Isabella reduced the authority of the Cortes and the *Hermandad*. Both declined as factors in the determination of national affairs. There were only nine meetings of this once powerful and influential national assembly during their reign, and although some important decisions were taken, the sessions were dominated and directed by the crown. Over a period of years the gradual deterioration of its authority resulted from the monarch's increasing independence of the Cortes in finances, made possible by the establishment of *impôts permanents,* or taxes that did not require the approval of the popular delegates. In contrast to the English Parliament, the Castilian assembly was less firmly rooted in the nation, with procurators coming from relatively few cities and with the absence of any strong ties with the country nobility. Consequently, in the final phase of the conflict for power, the burgher class and the rural aristocracy could not present a united front to their aggressive enemy. Toward the municipal league the attitude of Isabella was likewise unfriendly. A new constitution of the *Hermandad,* published by the Cortes of Madrigal in 1476 at the Queen's wish, reorganized the body in accordance with the plan of control. At length, in 1498, considering that it no longer served a purpose in inforcing the law and in the suppression of banditry, the crown ordered the abolition of the governing council of the *Hermandad.* Little restraint on the development of royal authority could thereafter be imposed by formal organizations representing civic interests.

We have alluded already to the fruitless and ineffectual protests of the municipalities in the fifteenth century against the encroachment of royal power. A final, and more resolute, attempt to turn back the absolutist trend of the times was made during the first years of the reign of the Emperor Charles V, the Catholic Rulers' grandson. Although the immediate cause of the revolt of the *comuneros,* as it was known, was the monarch's levy of taxes, particularly the *alcabala,* or sales tax, and a three-year papal tithe—the latter being deemed necessary because of his acceptance of the crown of the Holy Roman Empire—there were other, deep-seated reasons. Many of the cities, desiring to regain lost rights and privileges, believed that the moment was auspicious to strike a blow in their behalf. Moreover, the Spanish people manifested an open hostility to a ruler, who, born in Flanders, exhibited favoritism toward foreigners by appointing some of them to key posts in the realm. Inasmuch as the revolution occurred when municipal life was taking shape in America, its outcome was to affect the development of the colonial organization. It seems relatively certain that the seriousness of the struggle, in which the prominent cities of Toledo, Zamora, Segovia, and Burgos participated, influenced the formation of the crown's policy toward the new units of government springing up in the West Indies.

At the outset the movement, headed by the city council of Toledo, had brief success, owing to the absence of the Emperor in the Germanies and the widespread appeal of the remonstrances. The royal council, at Charles' behest, temporized until a favorable moment arrived for crushing the revolt. Accordingly, the government abolished the *servicio,* or the grant from the Cortes, collected the royal dues by methods used during the reign of Ferdinand and Isabella, and made some reforms in the administration of justice—in reality, concessions of slight consequence and of little duration. It cannot be said that they represented to any appreciable degree a return to the former age of municipal greatness. Propitious circumstances soon enabled the crown to gather the requisite forces for the ultimate suppression of the revolt. The royal cause was bolstered before long by the adhesion of aristocratic and bourgeois groups in many cities, who were alienated by the clamor of the masses for the abolition or reduction of class privileges. Rivalries and dissensions among the leaders of the insurrectionary army weakened its resistance, so that the stage was set for the downfall of the popular cause at the decisive battle of Villalar, April 23, 1521.

For the future position of the municipalities in the constitutional structure of Castile the revolt spelled the final effort of representative elements to withstand the ominous pressure of absolutism and autocracy. Thereafter the crown had easy sailing and encountered few storms in home waters. The scope of the disturbance indicated that there was latent discontent and opposition to the growing centralized authority and that the municipalities clung to their aspirations for civic freedom despite the repressive acts and measures of the Catholic Kings and their predecessors. But the military defeat extinguished these hopes, and the Emperor after 1521 not only dominated the city governments but extended his power over the Cortes, whose delegates were named by royal decree.

The *comuneros* movement had a bearing likewise on the character of the municipal organizations arising in the newly founded settlements in America. The civil conflict disclosed a partial flux in the relationship of the political institutions of the kingdom notwithstanding the great tendency toward concentration of authority in the crown's agencies, a constitutional vagueness and incertitude that may account in some measures for the absence of a clearly defined policy for the local entities evolving across the Atlantic. The gravity of the uprising counseled a cautious attitude in the extension of the principle of absolutism. These considerations, reinforced by the realization on the part of the Emperor and his advisors that colonization would be accelerated by liberal grants and concessions, resulted in the temporary enjoyment of certain prerogatives of self-government by the Spanish towns and cities in the Indies. On the whole it was a freer existence than that possessed by their contemporary counterparts on the Iberian peninsula. Unquestionably, this freedom would have lasted for a longer space of time had the decision at Villalar been otherwise. Possibly it would have been enduring.

8

GEORGE KUBLER

THE MENDICANT
CONTRIBUTION

Spain's conquest of America involved more than the simple imposition of a new ruling class and its institutions upon the Indian societies it subjugated. Along with the physical conquest, there was what Robert Ricard has termed the "spiritual conquest" undertaken by the Mendicant friars. The ideas and attitudes with which they approached this task, the prior experiences they drew upon, as well as the unconscious burden of rural culture and the outlook of Erasmian humanism they brought with them, are all detailed and explained in this selection from George Kubler's profound study of Mexican architecture and its cultural background.

After receiving his Ph.D. from Yale in 1940, George Kubler remained to teach, and he now holds the Robert Lehman Professorship in the Department of the History of Art. His interests and research, however, have ranged over a far wider field than his

From George Kubler, *Mexican Architecture of the Sixteenth Century*, 2 vols. (New Haven, Conn.: Yale University Press, 1948), I, 3–15. Reprinted by permission of the author.

title would suggest. He has published important
monographs on Peruvian demography, as well as
various studies in colonial Latin American history. In
1948–1949 he was the representative of the Smith-
sonian Institute in Peru, and from 1951 to 1956 he
headed the UNESCO Mission on the Restoration of
the Inca capital of Cuzco. Some of the more impor-
tant among his many publications are: The Religious
Architecture of New Mexico, The Art and Architecture of Ancient America, *and* The Shape of Time:
Remarks on the History of Things.

The Mendicant Orders, Franciscan, Dominican, and Augustinian, planned the towns, built the churches, governed
the communities, and educated the Indians. Organized
during the religious revival of the late Middle Ages, the
institutes of the Mendicant friars all specified the practice
of poverty and a return to the life of Christ and the
Apostles. Their great differences from the monastic orders
of an earlier Christianity appeared in preaching activity
among urban populations, and in renunciation both of
monastic retreat and of the wealth of the secular clergy. In
Mexico their missionary foundations and educational
establishments were the centers of the emergent patterns of
colonial culture.

Although the friars were assisted by Crown grants, and
by the encomenderos, who were ordered after 1536 to
support the religious foundations within their jurisdictions,
the true source of Mendicant power lay, of course, not in
its financial backing, but in the autocratic privileges accorded under *patronato real* of the Church in America. By
this institution (1508) the Papacy conceded radical privileges to the Spanish Crown, including the collection of
tithes and the fundamental right of presenting or nominat-
ing the candidates for all benefices in the American colony.
The Crown, at the insistence of Cortés, elected the Mendicants to fulfill the mission. By special dispensation, members of the regular clergy were permitted to be ordained as

parish priests. Thus the Crown confirmed the Mendicants in the exercise of total authority.

Patronato real led to certain abuses. Grave consequences resulted from the crippling of episcopal authority; the Church tended to become the instrument of the royal rather than the pontifical will; the litigiousness of the clergy was encouraged; the financial structure of the Church in America was held in tutelage, and the long periods *sede vacante* in the bishoprics provoked many disorders. But the power of the missionaries in their jurisdictions was unlimited save by the human weakness of the missionary himself. Labor could be impressed without pay. Recalcitrants were whipped or imprisoned. As early as 1533, the municipal council of the City of Mexico complained to the King that Franciscans had arrogated civil authority, interfering with justice and holding prisoners on their own initiative. At Ocuituco before 1541, conditions were so bad that the Augustinians were replaced by a curate.

In short, the authority of the Mendicants was practically absolute, and, equally important, it was buttressed by spiritual imperatives of an apostolic intensity. Civilian immigrants were incapacitated for the labors of a sound colonization by the administrative frustration of their absolute, Roman sense of private property. The weakening of this drive to action did not affect the regular clergy. On the contrary, the Mendicant vows of renunciation, the Christian doctrine of a compassionate deity, and the institutional authority of the sacraments were for a time masterfully supported by the Crown. The agrarian collectivism of the native peoples of America was ideal material within which to realize the Christian community. In the effort the missionary drew closer to the Indians than to his fellow-Europeans, against whom he held the Indians in protective custody until the time of their spiritual and temporal maturity should have arrived. The moral aims of all three Orders were identical; differences manifested themselves in the ways and means of their work.

The Mendicant evangelization of Mexico began in ear-
nest with the arrival of twelve Franciscans in 1524. The
Dominicans followed in 1526, and the Augustinians in
1533. As a whole, the pattern of Mendicant activity was
defined and established by the Franciscans. The Apostolic
Twelve, under the leadership of Martín de Valencia, rapidly penetrated among the great centers of Indian settlement. The first Bishop of Mexico, fray Juan de Zumárraga, was a Franciscan. The Franciscan missionaries early
established the widest and closest network of foundations,
covering the vast triangle of Mexico from Durango to
Tampico and Tehuantepec. It is therefore to the Franciscans that we must look for some definition of the
spiritual drives animating Mendicant activity.

Singularly little has been written about the European
antecedents of the Apostolic Twelve. Writers upon the subject have always assumed that the men were simple Franciscans, and that their motives were identical with those of
other Franciscans elsewhere in the world. The failure to
examine the European preparation of the men under
Martín de Valencia, and of fray Juan de Zumárraga in
particular, has prevented students from perceiving the re-
formist and Humanist training of this extraordinary troop
of Mendicant radicals.

These men were exalted by a spiritual unrest closely akin
to that of the Northern Reformation in Europe. Their story
may be said to reach its European climax with the re-
formatory action of Cardinal Ximénez de Cisneros before
1510. Confessor to Queen Isabella after 1492, Franciscan
Provincial in Castile, Archbishop of Toledo, Primate of
Spain, Inquisitor General after 1507, twice regent, founder
of the University of Alcala, and instigator of the Polyglot
Bible, Cisneros was one of the pre-Reformation protag-
onists of the Humanist *Philosophia Christi* in Europe. As
Bataillon has pointed out, Cisneros sought to achieve the
purification of the clergy by strengthening the preaching
mission and austerity of the Mendicant Orders. How this

latter was achieved, we shall see in a moment. Among the Franciscans, he favored the Observance against the lax Conventual branch of the Order. Similar internal movements of reform appeared *ca.* 1500 among Dominicans, Benedictines, and Jeronymites. Hence an enormous increase in reformed Mendicant population occurred in Cisneros' lifetime, an increase that Bataillon has related to the formation of a spiritual militia in the New World. To Cisneros' action, Bataillon also attributes the emergence of a spiritual elite of evangelical tendency, that would sympathize with Erasmus, and come under suspicion of Lutheranism later in the century. Bataillon says this *avant garde* of Catholicism in Spain has profound affinities with the Protestant Reformation. In particular, the reform movement among the Franciscan Observants was the central phenomenon, in a widespread cult of austerity to which Cardinal Cisneros gave administrative and political form.

The origins of the rift between Conventuals and Observants show in events of the lifetime of St. Francis. Such factions were the Italian Cesarenes after 1289, and many other Observant movements reaffirming the original Franciscan renunciation of property. After the mid-fourteenth century, such tendencies of Observant reform were powerfully impelled by the epidemics and secular disorders of the age. Separate branches increased greatly throughout Europe, such as the Coletani in Cologne and Saxony; the Clarenes in Umbria and Ancona; the Amadeists in Rome; the Neutri, the Caperolani, the Celestines, Martinianists, Narbonenses, Gentiles, etc. In 1506, Julius II ordered these many minor reforms to ally themselves either with the Conventual or the Observant branch of the Order, and to discontinue their separate existences.

In Spain, the history of the Regular Observance is most complicated, especially in its late fifteenth-century stages. Originating as a separate movement, the Spanish return to the strict rule of St. Francis was nominally complete by 1517, when no Conventual house was left in Spain. The special group from which Mexico later drew her friars, was founded in 1487 by fray Juan de la Puebla, and came to be known as the Minorites of the Blessed John of Puebla.

Known in secular life as the Count of Belalcazar, John of Puebla (born 1453) became a Jeronymite in 1476, but gained Sixtus IV's permission to change to the Italian Observance in 1480, when he was received at Subiaco near Assisi. Returning to Spain in 1487 with three Italian friars, to assume his nephew's guardianship, he organized a new reform, the Custodia de los Angeles, with the permission of the General Chapter of the Observance, held in Touraine in 1489. Two houses were founded, one near Hornachuelos in the Sierra Morena of Andalusia, called S. Maria de los Angeles, in 1490, and the other in 1493 at Belalcazar, where the Blessed John died in 1495. Among the purposes of the reform the friars acted to ameliorate the condition of the sparsely settled mountain dwellers of Andalusia, whose religious education had long been neglected for want of priests. In addition, the rule by which the custody was governed prescribed extreme poverty and spiritual retreat. Each week, four friars were selected to go into four separate hermitages, for one week each. At the entrance to the refectory, these friars kissed the feet of all the other friars in the establishment. In retreat, silence was observed, and the friars ate nothing cooked or alive, abstaining even from milk products, disciplining themselves thrice daily, and relieved only from the general obligation to manual labor. The Custodia ultimately included fourteen foundations, when it was incorporated as the Provincia de los Angeles in 1518.

After the Blessed John's death, his disciple Juan de Guadalupe (born 1450), wishing to extend the reform to the province of Granada, introduced an even severer rule. Hence, although John of Puebla is often taken as the spiritual father of the Discalced or Barefoot movement in the Observance, many incline to credit Juan de Guadalupe with the definitive formulation of this way of life. In creating the *Observantia strictissima*, Guadalupe introduced the pointed cape, short mantle, patched robe, and barefoot practice that were later to be taken over by the Discalced and Capuchin friars. The members of his reform assumed the name of Minorites of the Holy Gospel. In 1496, they secured release from Observant jurisdiction, and proceeded, first to convert the Moslems of Granada, and then to found hermitages at Oropesa and Plasencia. Later foundations were made, after 1500, near Trujillo and in Portugal. Guadalupe and his followers made a practice of preaching an austere and simple Christianity to the spiritually neglected peasants and townsfolk of the western provinces. In such endeavors, the friars prepared unconsciously for the great evangelical mission that was to become theirs in 1523.

Meanwhile the Observants took alarm at the scores of recruits flocking to Juan de Guadalupe. In 1502, after several earlier efforts, they secured a brief from Alexander VI, revoking Guadalupe's privileges as accorded by the same pope in 1496. The reforming friars then were expelled from their Castilian houses, and took refuge in Portugal. Guadalupe died in 1506, but his followers succeeded in securing papal permission to found new establishments. Returning to Castile, they found their houses in Trujillo (N.S. de la Luz) and Salvaleon (Montesion) ruined, and met further persecution from the Observants, because of an earlier allegiance given to the Conventual branch of the Order, precisely in order to escape Observant jurisdiction. Julius II finally accorded them provincial status in 1508, with two *Custodias,* the Piedad in Portugal, and the Santo Evangelio in Castile. The two custodies then met pressure by the Chapter General of the Franciscans to join either the Conventuals or the Regular Observance. For strategic reasons, the Portuguese custody became Observant, and the Castilian custody continued its alliance with the Conventuals. In 1517, upon the initiative of Leo X, all the reforming branches once again considered the choice of aligning with the Observants or the Conventuals. Provincial status was given both custodies, in Portugal and Castile, and both threw in their lot with the Observance.

The Castilian group became the Province of S. Gabriel, and the Portuguese beçame the Province of Piedad. At about the same time, the followers of John of Puebla formed another province, under the advocacy of N.S. de los Angeles.

Hence the remarkably severe reform inaugurated by John of Puebla ultimately found expression in three separate provinces, of which none really wished to be identified with either the Conventuals or the Observants, but only to maintain the integrity of its preaching mission and austerity of retreat, independently of all institutional interference.

With one or another of those *Observantias strictissimas*, all members of the Apostolic Twelve and many friars of the other early missions show intimate connection. They participated in the desperate struggle for autonomy and jurisdictional independence, and they spent their lives as friars within the reform, before their departure to America. Significantly enough, they adopted the name of the Castilian custody, the Santo Evangelio, when naming their Mexican territory, in honor of the custody that had been absorbed by the Regular Observants as the Province of S. Gabriel in 1517. It is again to be stressed that the reformed groups in Spain and Portugal worked among neglected rural and village folk, and that the friars' privileges expressly conceded their status as *predicadores apostólicos*, in order that, in the words of the bull issued by Alexander VI in 1496, they might "throughout the world among the faithful and the infidel, preach the word of God and the Holy Gospel." In such terms was it possible for the reforming Franciscans to prepare for their American mission, by defining a labor of evangelization in Europe itself, that none of their Franciscan colleagues would undertake. The rule established by Juan de Guadalupe is by far the more important, in that he originally worked in the newly-conquered province of Granada, among the Moslem farmers and townspeople who had no other religious attentions. Here, then, is the specific preparation for the American work, among a non-European people in Spain itself, in the territory designated as the Custodia del Santo Evangelio.

The Apostolic mission of the Twelve was very clearly present to the authorities and to the friars themselves. Their number explicitly appears in 1523, at the time of their appointment, as twelve, "quoniam hic fuit numerus discipulorum Christi."[1] The plan probably comes from the General of the Order, Francisco de Quiñones, who later became the Cardinal de Santa Cruz. Quiñones himself wished to go to the Indies, and in effect, received the permission of Leo X on April 25, 1521. Later, in 1526, he wished to take charge of the entire missionary enterprise in America, in the spirit of the primitive Apostolic Church. The plan remained the constant obsession of his later career. But Quiñones was an anti-Erasmian in his dealings with Charles V and the Papacy, even if he advanced the Cisnerian pre-Reformation by his belief that Christianity might revive through the strict Franciscan Observance.

In any event, it was Quiñones, who, when attending the chapter meeting of Province of S. Gabriel at Belvis in 1523, ordered Martín de Valencia to take his following and go forth upon the Mexican mission. Fray Martín was the first provincial elected in S. Gabriel, taking office in 1518, and insisting upon an extreme severity of discipline in the houses of the Province. In 1523, the Province had but one hundred seventy-five friars in eleven *conventos,* from which fray Martín drew his Apostolic band. Without exception, every one of the twelve had taken refuge in the reform group from the lax and secular life of conventual establishments elsewhere; indeed one of them, Alonso Suárez, quite like Martín de Valencia, once entertained the thought of becoming a Carthusian in the quest for a greater severity of rule. Both Martín de Valencia and Andrés de Cordova, furthermore, were disciples of Juan de Guadalupe. It was a tightly knit, radical little band of men who had worked together for many years as apostolic

---

[1] ". . . because this was the number of Christ's disciples." (Ed.)

preachers and in the intention of effecting great conversions. By 1543, the fame of their work was proclaimed by Alonso de Isla in the following words,

> I do believe that it stands with them as it did in the primitive church, as we read in the Acts of the Apostles [2, 44] where it is said, "And all that believed were together; and had all things common." It does not seem to be otherwise in these [countries] converted and taught by the twelve apostolic friars.

Thus the grand program of Cardinal Cisneros came to realization, beyond even his intentions, carried by the obscure friars from western Spain. But in 1524, the Franciscan missionaries were not, to our knowledge, in contact with the political and religious thought of North European Humanism. If the Apostolic Twelve represented Cisnerian Spain, a later group of missionaries under Juan de Zumárraga represented Erasmian thought in Mexico.

In 1527, the year of Zumárraga's nomination by Charles V as first Bishop of Mexico, the court of Spain carried on an extraordinary discussion of the work and philosophy of Erasmus. The powerful Chancellor, Gattinara, not only read Erasmus, but was aided in Latin correspondence by Alonso de Valdes, the great admirer of Erasmus. Erasmus' name was again much discussed, when the monastic orders undertook to demonstrate errors in Erasmus' writings; in March, 1527, their presentation before the Grand Inquisitor oddly took the form of strong praise. Not only was the Emperor favorably disposed towards Erasmus, but the Archbishop of Toledo and the Grand Inquisitor followed the paths of admiration laid out by Cardinal Cisneros. The Conference of Valladolid, held in June and July, brought Erasmus' writings under close scrutiny by large numbers of his supporters and enemies in Spain. As Bataillon has shown in great detail, these events precipitated the "Erasmian invasion" of Spain after 1527. For our purposes, it is important that the Emperor spent Holy Week in the monastery at Abrojo, near Valladolid. This monastery, in the strict Observant province of Concepción, had Zumárraga as its guardian at that moment, following his term of office as Provincial (1520–1526). The Emperor's attention was first drawn to Zumárraga by his charity and austerity, and Zumárraga accepted an Inquisitorial commission to punish the sorcerers of Biscaya, whose language and customs he knew well as a native of Durango. His nomination to the see of Mexico came at the end of 1527. It is this friar who has been listed with the Grand Inquisitor Manrique, Archbishop Fonseca, Bishop Cabrero, Archibishop Merino, and Alonso Ruiz de Virues, as among the outstanding Erasmian prelates of Spain in the reign of Charles V. As Zumárraga was born *ca.* 1461, it is likely that he became aware of the thought of Erasmus long before his episcopal nomination. Unfortunately, his early biography is unknown, but several events in his Mexican career indicate an audacious and radical policy of action, founded upon the *Philosophia Christi* promulgated by Erasmus and diffused throughout the literate world of Spain by 1525.

The main documents of Zumárraga's contact with Spanish Erasmianism are the doctrinal books printed in Mexico under his direction, and a copy of More's *Utopia* and Erasmus' *Epigrammata* in his possession. . . . The *Doctrina breve* purported to instruct the priests of the Mexican diocese. From Erasmus' *Enchiridion* Zumárraga adapted the chapters upon the remedies against vices; and the *Paraclesis* yielded the conclusion. In compiling the little work, Zumárraga availed himself of the modified translation by Alonso Fernández de Madrid (Arcediano del Alcor). In general, Zumárraga departed from Erasmus in insisting upon the gentility of the Platonic, Stoic, and Pythagorean philosophers. He changed Erasmus' *Filosofía cristiana* to "doctrina cristiana," and deleted the name of Erasmus, but confirmed the denunciation of scholasticism. Zumárraga also approved Erasmus' advocacy of the unlimited diffusion of Scripture, as in the *Paraclesis,* and kept the doctrine of interior Christianity intact. On the whole, the Pauline formulas of Charity appear as in the *Enchiri-*

dion. The unfavorable remarks about Mendicants were, of course, suppressed.

The *Doctrina cristiana,* on the other hand, was prepared as a catechism for Indian use. It rests upon the *Suma de doctrina christiana* by Dr. Constantino Ponce de la Fuente, confessor to Charles V, and head of the so-called "Lutheran" movement in Seville. This little summary of essential Christianity, conceived in the spirit of Erasmus, insists upon the primacy of faith over works. It had a wide distribution in Spain, appearing in at least five editions between 1543 and 1551. When Zumárraga authorized its printing in Mexico, it was enriched by a conclusion drawn again from the *Paraclesis.*

Zumárraga's own copy of Erasmus' *Epigrammata* is the Froben edition of 1518, which contains More's *Utopia.* In the two sections of the English humanist's book, two contrasting worlds intersect: the world of Henry VIII with its gross inequalities and the depredations of court and clergy; and the ideal world of humanism. A Lucianic irony enhances the contrast—England and Utopia mirror one another in reversed and opposite images; England's misery and the serenity of Utopia in More's intention, represent actual and possible worlds, perhaps in the relation of nightmare—from which the sleeper will awake—to reality.

For the Mexican humanists, such complexities in the English political situation were irrelevant. They attended only to the possible and ideal world of Utopia. The marginal notations to the *Utopia* are nearly all in the same rapid hand, and bear an unmistakable resemblance to Zumárraga's known holographs. Zumárraga's notations show him especially sensitive to More's remarks upon the foolish estimation of gold, upon crafts and hospitals, social organization, and religious exercises. They are the notes of a straightforward, simple man of action, revealing a decidedly naive curiosity about the natural and historical identification of Utopia, as on p. 63, where he glosses More's navigational distances. Zumárraga failed to comment upon More's esthetics, or his speculations on health and the pleasures of the mind. Significantly, there is no comment upon the passages treating of war and religious tolerance, but much upon the industry of Utopians (one marginal note reads "none is idle"), the manner of dying, the laws, the forms of religious community, the size of the *familia* ("30 families eat together"), the status of priests, and the form of towns, where Zumárraga has underlined the passages describing Utopian architecture with heavy, rapid, agitated strokes.

We are still ignorant of the main details of Zumárraga's spiritual biography. Was he an "Erasmianizing" prelate before leaving Spain in 1528, or did he come under Erasmus' influence after beginning his American mission? Were fray Andrés de Olmos, the linguist, and fray Juan de Alameda, the builder, chosen to accompany him in 1527, from among a circle of humanist friars in the Provincia de la Concepción? How long before 1540 did Zumárraga's intention to mediate the *Philosophia Christi* to Indians take shape in his mind? The answers to these and many other questions lie in the conventual archives of Spain.

One incident in Franciscan recruitment for the Mexican mission deserves mention. In 1532, at the General Chapter of the Regular Observance held in Toulouse, letters from Martín de Valencia and Juan de Zumárraga arrived, asking for missionaries to work in the Indies. The Latin letters at once appeared in French and German, the latter in several editions, and thus circulated widely throughout Europe. The date and place of promulgation are significant. In the 1530's Toulouse was among the foremost university cities of the world, especially in jurisprudence; extravagantly pious, with a pan-European population. It was also the scene of great religious unrest. Between 1528 and 1532, evangelical ideas had spread among the university students, and scriptural studies were secretly conducted in the Augustinian monastery. An inquisitorial trial brought the discovery of a religious movement throughout southwestern France. Its leader, Jean de Cahors, was burned alive in 1532, and decrees of arrest were issued against some forty students, friars, and professors of law. The moment coincides with the most active recruitment of friars by the Franciscan mission in Mexico, and it suggests that an investigation of the European antecedents of the many dozens of Franciscans arriving in Mexico after 1532 would throw much light upon the religious motivation of the Mexican mission.

Similar uncertainties surround the biography of the first Bishop of Michoacan, Vasco de Quiroga, Zumárraga's friend, and the disciple of Thomas More. About Quiroga we know nothing between 1492 and 1530, and yet, as Zavala has shown, he was one of the most effective agents of humanist Christianity in Mexico. In 1531, the Audiencia commissioned him to establish a center for the Indians just released from monastic schools. The object was to provide a place of passage between the atmosphere of the schools and the still pagan environment of the Indians' families. The settlement, called Santa Fe, was later duplicated upon the north shore of Lake Patzcuaro. The special interest of these communities is that they are the earliest manifestations now known in Mexico, of Humanist and Erasmian ideas of social reform, for Zumárraga's catechisms did not appear until the mid-1540's. Quiroga stated explicitly in later life that he had patterned his towns upon More's *Utopia*, of which a copy was in the possession of his friend, Zumárraga. The municipal ordinances composed by Quiroga before 1565 also reveal the closest affinities with the social thought of Thomas More. An interesting estimate of the character of Quiroga comes from the pen of his colleague, the Oidor Salmerón, who wrote in 1531, that Quiroga was "virtuous and most solicitous for the welfare of the Indians; but timid and scrupulous, therefore more apt to carry out orders than to give them." It is the familiar judgment made at all times of idealists by their busy colleagues. But the unsolved question immediately arises, whether Quiroga was acting upon his own initiative, or "carrying out orders" of the Audiencia when he founded the Utopian Sante Fe.

Thus the two Franciscans, Martín de Valencia and Juan de Zumárraga, and the humanist lawyer, Vasco de Quiroga, carried to New Spain the idealist social and religious theory of their day. The part played by the Augustinians and the Dominicans is less well known. That the Cisnerian reform, if not the *Philosophia Christi*, extended to the other Mendicant Orders in Spain, has been suggested, but not demonstrated in detail. Among the Dominicans, an Observant movement took form at the close of the fifteenth century, in the foundation of new houses at Granada, Avila, and Valladolid. The head of the first Dominican mission to Mexico in 1526, Domingo de Betanzos, was an austere exponent of monastic reform. Born *ca.* 1480, he resolved, when still a student of law at Salamanca, to become a hermit. After examining the conditions at the monastery of Montserrat, he rejected the thought of becoming a Benedictine and continued to Rome. Upon an island near Naples, he withdrew in eremitic retreat for five years. Returning to Spain, he took the Dominican habit in 1510, and applied for passage to Hispaniola in 1515, where he is reported to have influenced Bartolomé de las Casas to enter the Order. In Mexico, Betanzos' policy was to introduce the strictest possible observance. He wished to establish twelve great conventos, each with thirty resident friars, who should go forth in pairs to administer the district. Although he never fully realized his desire, Betanzos, as much as Martín de Valencia, may be regarded as an instrument of the Cisnerian reform.

The internal history of the Spanish Augustinians at this period still remains obscure. A reformed or Observant branch of the Order was introduced into Spain in 1430 by Juan de Alarcón. By 1505, its houses were so numerous that a division into four provinces was necessary—New Castile, Old Castile, León, and Andalusia. The strict Observance of the Discalced or Recollect Augustinians did not come to Spain until 1588. For our purposes, the most striking figure in the Augustinian mission of Mexico was fray Alonso de la Vera Cruz. Educated at Alcala, in the University founded by Cardinal Cisneros, and under Francisco de Vitoria at Salamanca, he was invited in 1535 by the head of the Mexican mission to accompany him to America, as a secular priest who would instruct the friars in arts and theology. Taking the Augustinian vows in Mexico in 1537, fray Alonso first worked among the Tarascans at Tiripitio. In 1542 Bishop Quiroga put him in charge of the diocese during Quiroga's contemplated absence in Spain. After a life of productive scholarship and vigorous missionary activity, fray Alonso was sent to Spain in 1562, and gained the favor of Philip II. Before returning to Mexico he became *Visitador y Reformador de los conventos del Reino de Toledo*. Escobar adds the interesting comment that this office was given him in order that he might introduce into Europe the stricter Augustinian Observance of America. That this Mexican Observance was not out of touch with Erasmian circles in Spain is revealed by the attitude of Alonso de la Vera Cruz, upon hearing of the arrest of fray Luis de León by the Inquisition. The Augustinian mystic . . . became the proponent of a veiled Erasmian illuminism,[2] and fray Alonso, when he learned the distressing news of fray Luis' arrest, spoke out before the assembled University in Mexico, saying that the Inquisition might burn him if they burned fray Luis, for he agreed with the manner of the propositions for which the poet had been arrested.

With respect to the other Mendicants in Mexico, moreover, the Augustinians displayed a radical humanism, insisting more upon the high moral capacity of the Indians than did their Franciscan and Dominican colleagues, and

---

[2] A doctrine which emphasized the direct communion of the soul with God in place of good works and the sacraments; considered heretical by orthodox Catholic theologians. (Ed.)

admitting the Indians to Communion and Extreme Unction, sacraments which the Franciscans sometimes refused the Indians. The late-coming Augustinians carried a Christian humanism that in certain respects reached far deeper than that of their Mendicant colleagues, in assuming the spiritual readiness of the Indians, and shortening their tutelage.

Hence it is fairly easy . . . to demonstrate that the intellectual leaders of the Mexican colonization were governed by the most novel religious and social ideas of their day in Spain, and that they formed a spiritual *avant garde* for the late Renaissance in America.

THREE

❁

THE ETHOS
OF MEDIEVAL
IBERIA

9

AMÉRICO CASTRO

THE SPANISH
SENSE OF NOBILITY

*Spain's relative backwardness and sense of unease in
the modern world has been a constant obsession of
Spanish intellectuals ever since the Generation of '98.
After numerous attempted explanations via analysis of
the "Spanish personality," some more recent thinkers
have turned instead to an examination of the Spanish
past in search of a more adequate answer. Among the
most prominent of these is Américo Castro, who finds
the peculiar national character of Spain to have been
formed in the period between the fall of the Visigothic
Empire (711) and the reign of Ferdinand and Isabella
(1479–1504). In the following selection he analyzes
the social and intellectual factors that he sees as
having created that quintessential Spanish type, the
hidalgo.*

*Américo Castro was born in Rio de Janeiro in 1885
and took his Ph.D. at the University of Madrid in
1911, where he remained to teach until 1936. With*

From Américo Castro, *The Structure of Spanish History*
(Princeton, N.J.: Princeton University Press, 1954), pp. 589–
592, 604–614, 628–635. Copyright 1954 by Princeton University Press. Reprinted by permission.

the outbreak of the Civil War he left Spain and, after a short residence in Buenos Aires, settled in the United States where he taught at Princeton University until recently. It was here that he summed up his lifelong reflections on la condición española *in his controversial book* España en su história, *translated into English under the title* The Structure of Spanish History. *Among his other publications are* Hacía Cervantes, El pensamiento de Cervantes *and numerous volumes of essays and literary criticism.*

The Iberian Christian arrived at the year 1500 with the awareness that he was facing immense and unsuspected possibilities. The sense of triumph over Moor and Jew after the events of 1492 made him feel secure in the plenitude of his power. The discovery of new worlds and the conquest of the kingdom of Naples indicated that the "beyonds" of his dreams were turning into close-by reality. The only requisite to fulfillment was to persevere in the traditional faith, to tense the will, and courageously defy death. "Men of high mettle, to whom was entrusted the honor of Spain" were vanquishing the troops of the king of France in Calabria and Naples by emulating the characters in the tales of Amadis and Palmerin. The path to international prestige and greatness was valor; and the humane virtues stood at the forefront: "The Great Captain commanded that the prisoners should be treated with magnificent generosity, and this was intended to bring honor and fame to the Spanish nation." "The Spaniards fought with such virility and spirit that it was a wonderful thing to see; and the French put into that battle [Seminara, 1503] all their hopes for a lustrous page in the chronicles of their king." But on this and many other occasions, victory went to the Spaniards.

The plowman, "from childhood destined by his fateful

star for the struggle and stubborn resistance of the hard earth," passed without transition from his clods to dominion over distant lands whose existence had only recently been suspected. "The ship departs on its journey from the sheltered ports of western Spain . . . following as best she can the will of her master, eager to lay his eyes on new things and strange peoples, and to ennoble his spirit, expecting to increase his worth by increasing his knowledge" (Torres Naharro, *Propalladia,* 1517). Lands and sea surrender meekly. In a brief span of years, Hispanic valor had girdled the planet's surface. There was a general awareness of all this, and the more gifted sensibilities expressed it in exquisite fashion, for arms and letters went together in intimate reciprocity. In Gil Vicente's *Auto de fama,* Castile and Portugal both aspire to possess Fame:

"Well you know, high lady, the victories of Castile. . . . You have heard that in our time she has conquered everything she sought to subjugate. . . . The Italian fields recount their Roman deeds. And Granada, won with such hard effort, is a wondrous thing."

But Castile, in Gil Vicente's words, recognized the preeminence of Portugal, "because her victories are in far-distant places and for the faith."

The Hispanic conquests were not shaped after any historic pattern. Rome had adjusted the peoples she conquered to institutions in which empire, law, and religion were unified. Spain's overseas enterprises from the outset established the never-before-heard-of-dispute as to whether the conquest was legitimate or not. The king, the church, and private individuals carried on debates, bloody at times, over their respective rights. One might have expected the common effort in imperial expansion to reduce the Iberian Peninsula to a compact unity, yet Castile, Portugal, and Aragon-Catalonia did not fuse into a single will. Thus, in the middle of the seventeenth century, when the invisible bonds that held the Iberian peoples together were loosened, Portugal, Catalonia, and even Aragon thought of breaking away from the peninsular union. Immediate interests were lacking to incite the units to common and coordinate efforts.

It is no less surprising that from the outset of the conquest of America it was the Spaniards themselves who incited the indigenous populations to rebel against Spain. This is the ultimate implication of the anarchic tendency, as we would say today, in the work of Father Las Casas. The Spaniard who lived in active opposition to the state within Spain also lived in conscious agony (*vivía desviviéndose*) as he confronted the fact of the domination of the Indians by the Spanish people. If ambition and avarice had been the only motives of the conquest, no one would have questioned the right of the conqueror. But Ercilla, in *La Araucana* (1569), shows his sympathy for the Araucanian Indian rebels. Before this, Antonio de Guevara had criticized Spanish imperialism in *El villano del danubio*. And Quevedo says: "Those who are gluttonous for provinces have always died of surfeit. . . . America is a rich and beautiful strumpet who was unfaithful to her spouses the Indians. . . . The Christians say that heaven has punished the Indies (*las Indias*) because they adore idols; and we Indians say that heaven is bound to punish the Christians because they adore Indian women (*las indias*)" (*La hora de todos,* 1638). The idea that it was vicious and wicked for the Spaniards to maintain themselves in their American dominions reappears in Cadalso: "The great treasures quickly acquired in the Indies distract many from cultivating the mechanical arts in the Peninsula and from increasing its population" (*Cartas marruecas,* III). In his *Noches lúgubres* the same author alludes to the gold that someone "brought to *tyrant Europe* from *unfortunate America.*" And other texts could be added. There is no need, therefore, to look around among ideas gestated outside Spain for motives and incitements for the independence of the Hispano-American colonies. The principal reason lay in the very process of Spanish history, within which Las Casas' strange form of Christianity turned eventually into rational criticism.

It was not in the pursuance of shrewdly calculated plans that the Spaniards spread over the world. If they had had any such plans, their undertakings would have had much more modest proportions. Some went out in search of riches, spices, and gold, as had the Venetians; for many converted Spanish Jews and Moors the primary impulse was to find a peace that they did not have at home; the religious missionaries reproduced in sixteenth-century America the pattern of the spiritual conquest of the Moslems; at their side were men eager to exercise personal seigniory in a peculiarly Hispanic form, to the end of "winning honor," creating for themselves halos of grandeur worthy of their nobility and their manly virtue. "Good men of noble aspiration must seek life and must go from the good thing to the better . . . and try to win honor," wrote Bernal Díaz del Castillo as he began his *History of the Conquest of New Spain,* reflecting the feeling of those who, after all, were the authentic conquistadors. The idea that avarice and cruelty were the only motives for Hispano-Portuguese expansion presupposes a total ignorance of the reality of history. All kinds of stars guided those men, whose spiritual energy came from a very special form of humanity in which strange fantasies and the most concrete realizations were harmonized. The territorial expansion of the Spaniards was something like a novel or a drama in which the characters actually lived and died, with no end save that of consuming themselves and expressing themselves in the tension of their own existence. It is symbolic, to begin with, that the two extremities of Spanish dominions in America should bear names taken from the romances of chivalry: California, from the *Sergas de Esplandián;* Patagonia, from *Primaleón.* In the center rises the incredible figure of Bishop Vasco de Quiroga, rigorously applying to the Mexican Indians everything that Thomas More imagined in his *Utopia.* To try to fit Spanish life only to economic and down to earth criteria is truly to waste time and not to understand history. Among the thousands who sailed from the "sheltered ports of western Spain," there were many, many indeed, who went looking for fantastic islands in the gloomy ocean, for giants and pygmies, the fountain of eternal youth, the seven enchanted cities, the virgin Amazons, the lake where the sun retired to sleep, the Golden King, or the footprints left by the Apostles. Eight hundred years of a life comparable to nothing else in Europe had made this and much more possible.

.   .   .

Let us now look still further back. . . . those who initiated the Reconquest—Galicians, Asturians, Cantabrians, Pyreneans from Navarre and Aragon—had no unity save that of the common purpose of their attacks against the Moslemry of the south, a unity counteracted by the lateral quarrels between one group of Christians and another. The centers of traditional culture within the Peninsula as well as those in foreign lands lay far away (Hispalis, Toletum, Caesar Augusta; Ireland, England, Byzantium, etc.). The Hispano-Christian of the eighth, ninth, and tenth centuries fashioned his life along the lines offered to him by occasional political weakness and the constant cultural superiority of the Islamic South. Sustained by his faith in the heavenly beyond and the incentive of Moorish riches, the Christian conquered lands and at the same time was molding his life within him. Three hundred years of continuous risk are a great many years. Living in the hope of having the nearby land and in the faith in Santiago and San Millán made the Christian feel as strong and as much a lord as his powerful enemy, whose spirit was also supported by a faith—in the Moslems' "if God wills" (*ojalá*) and in the Jews' "so be it" (amen).

The outward sign of this lack of adhesion to a stable present was the absence of a capital to serve as a center for all the Christians, whose lives opened toward the future promise of the conquest: "there," not "here," the magnificent, ideal capital was to be found. The rationalist French centered this history in the fixed point of their capital city,

Paris, whereas the Hispanic capitals varied and shifted till 1560, a fact which reveals the migratory, frontier spirit of a people who existed in and for the land camp-ground of their history. The *reconquistadore's* life was a waiting for the call to war, the *apellido* that sent him forth to a distant horizon. The only sure, unshakeable thing in him was his conscious experience of feeling himself as all readiness for a mission, for something that would befall him. He was born to life with the certainty of already being what he ought to be; the rest was a matter of time and confidence, just as the nobleman's son had every expectation of becoming a full-fledged nobleman when he reached the age for putting on armor. The foundation stone of all that was Hispanic was the feeling that one was the son of God or the "son of *algo*" (*fijodalgo*). It was enough to embark upon the ship of destiny, with its sails set for a beyond open to everyone: "God grant you good fortune, for you have no need of knowledge." Hence the Hispanic people's deep-seated feeling for the individual person and their sense of "caste," founded on a constitution which, since it is eternal, has never been written, and therefore escapes the critical action of temporal changes. Spanish democratism is at the opposite pole from the democracy based on "the rights of man," a rational construction that has never entered the Spaniard's head nor his life.

It is hardly necessary to say that the contents of Hispanic history have not been the same as those of the history of Israel, although it is at the same time undeniable that for the Semites as well as Hispanians the quest for truth has had meaning only when it has affected their conscious experience of their existence and the conduct of their life. The celebrated medical science of the Spanish Jews was concerned more with the avoidance of ills to come than with present complaints. Their knowledge of the stars did not grow out of a desire for scientific knowledge of the structure of the universe but rather was aimed at how the stars influenced the lives of men. The Spaniards realized titanic and beautiful achievements in the lands that they discovered and colonized with the intention of honoring their faith and of honoring themselves as sons of God and as noblemen by nature. They left to others the preoccupation with discovering the physico-chemical properties of American cocaine and quinine, or with the cultivation of the potato. Such tasks did not interest those seekers after eternity. It had to be this way, given the possibilities of the "dwelling place" of Hispanic life—the *vividura,* possibilities that were clearly perceived by the more intelligent. Witness Feijóo in the eighteenth century: "It must be confessed that physics and mathematics are almost foreigners in Spain" (*Teatro crítico,* iv, 14). And following in Feijóo's footsteps, Father Isla recognized that "in Portugal and even in all of Spain, there is scarcely any awareness of what real Physics is. . . . There has not appeared, nor is there likely to appear, for a long time, anyone who will study it and advance it, for before this can be done, many obstacles must be overcome, and in the national genius these are little less than invincible" (*Fray Gerundio,* Book II, Chap. 6).

In the fifteenth century things could not be said so plainly, but indirectly the poverty of Hispano-Christian thought was recognized in the fact that when anyone set about making an inventory of Hispanic learning, only Moslem and Jewish thinkers could be cited. Fernán Pérez de Guzmán can recall only Averroes and Maimonides:

"And the Commentary [on Aristotle] of the pagan Avén Ruiz, pleases us. . . . If the Hispanic realm recalls the Egyptian sage Rabbi Moysén [Maimonides], it will plainly see that not for nothing was Cordova called another Athens. . . ."

It is significant that the name of Averroes was Hispanized as *Avén Ruiz,* revealing that the Spaniards felt him to be one of their own, and it is on him that Pérez de Guzmán bases his pride as a Cordovan. (The Duke of Rivas was to do the same thing in the nineteenth century in *El moro expósito*). Spain, "always rich in martial spirits" (says Feijóo) and in energetic propagandists for her belief

(Domingo de Guzmán, Vicente Ferrer, Ignacio de Loyola), reached the sixteenth century with the conscious conviction that she deserved all the promises that a propitious future might offer her, but with no exploitable wealth save that of her agriculture and the immense potential energy in the strong-willed spirit of her men. It seems evident to me, nevertheless, that without the *deux ex machina* of American riches, Spain would have been unable to maintain her European empire, or even to affirm herself as a self-ruled nation.

The Jews' help had been inestimable. Living as an intermediary between Moors and Christians, they presented an "occidental" aspect impossible in the Moslem. Gifted in languages, hard-working, peripatetic, and always alert, they articulated with the Christian much more than with the Moor. The special character of their occupations, either inaccessible or contemptible for the Christian, converted them into a caste, since their different belief prevented them from gradually uniting with the Christians, who really formed likewise not another class, but a different caste. The tolerance of the Middle Ages and the intermingling of three incompatible creeds hindered the establishment of the graduated regimen that prevailed in European feudalism—peasants, artisans, nobles, clergy. Spanish society broke up into three different hierarchies, each independent of the others, and therein lies the explanation for the absence of a feudal society. If, as we have seen, there were still in the fourteenth century Moors and Jews who held castles in fief from the king, what kind of well-ordered hierarchy could be organized on such a base?

But it is not only the fact (which might be an accident) that there were Hebrew bailiffs in Aragon or Moorish and Jewish wardens in the castles of Castile that stood in the way of feudal organization in Spain. It is the meaning of the facts that explains history, not the facts, which are in themselves mere inert appearance. Life, individual as well as collective, goes on in obedience to one hierarchy or another of values. Otherwise human life is inconceivable. And so, the Hispano-Christian, with no other horizon than his beliefs, could not organize within the Christian community the whole of his system of values. He had to accept as inescapable realities various kinds of Moslem and Jewish superiority. Thus, the daughter of James II of Aragon, married to the highest lord of Castile, brought up her children under the tutelage of Jews. . . . The Christian found himself in a situation of cultural colonialism and no more so nor less than did the Spanish Moors and Jews, whose place in one hierarchy was below and in another above that of the Christians. In contrast to Spain, the feudalism of Western Christianity had a tightly homogeneous hierarchic scale of respect, submission, privilege and duty. The lord constituted a total and absolute horizon for the vassal. The Spaniard, quite the contrary, had to divide his loyalties among three different authorities (Christian, Moslem, Jewish), with no clear sense of what was owed to Caesar and what to God. In this situation, feudalism of the European type became impossible.

We have seen how useless it was to pass laws preventing the Christians from utilizing the good services of Jews and Moors. The tolerant laws of the *Partidas* (which in any case was a purely theoretical code in the thirteenth century) accepted the existence of Moors and Jews, but they did not suggest that the Christians should bow before their occasional superiority. The Jews were tolerated so that "they would live as in captivity forever, and would be a reminder to men that they came of the lineage of those who crucified Our Lord Jesus Christ" (*Partidas*, VII, 24, 2). Christian life was therefore the product of an inevitable custom and a disregarded legal will. Logically, this was a senseless contradiction; but since the Christian kingdoms of Spain lived this way for more than five centuries, such an easy description as "senseless contradiction" would seem inadequate, and it would be more worthwhile to think that the form of life consisted in an inescapable compromise between two beliefs, between believing that the Jew was a deicide and believing that it was legitimate to accept him. The synagogue was also a house of God, according to the *Partidas*.

By accepting the occasional superiority of his unfaithful fellow-citizens, the Christian was deprived of his consciousness of being lord of his land. The Christian did not believe in his own superiority for the same reasons as the nobility of feudal Europe—not, that is, because he was doing what the commoner could not do (noblesse oblige) —but because he was possessed of a better belief. This explains why the Christian had more a sense of caste than of class. The social class bases its rank on what it does; the rank of the caste depends on the mere existence of the person: in the last analysis, all the Hispano-Christians ended up by feeling themselves a superior caste by virtue of the fact that they were Christians and not Moors or Jews. The form of their daily existence, then, was analogous to that of their literary creation: a personal "integralism" Islamico-Judaic in root and serving as a vital common denominator to Moors, Jews, and Christians.

The two subject castes were joined to the political superior caste by means of what one might call a broken scale of values. That is, deeds and accomplishments were seen as valuable while those who performed them were held in low esteem. Artisans, businessmen, technologists, scholars, etc., produced all manner of good things, but these products were tainted from birth by the fact that their producers came from castes deemed inferior; and no matter how good the products were, the producers *were not converted into a legitimate social class*. The production of wealth did not become an index of value for the Christian caste, which both needed and scorned those who built up fortunes. In the absence of such an attitude, the hermetic caste of the Christians would have been broken and the infidel castes would have infiltrated it, thus endangering its existence as the ruling caste. Social functions had to be differentiated not according to their objective value but according to the castes that carried them out.

The tailor (*alfayate*), the barber (*alfajeme*), the muleteer (*harriero*), the mason (*albañil*), the architect (*alarife*), the inspector of weights and measures (*almotacén*), the shoemaker (*zapatero*), etc., were Moors. The tax-gatherer (*almojarife*), the physician, the pharmacist, the veterinary (*albéitar*), the tradesman, the astrologer, the interpreter (*trujamán*), and other such were Jews. The Christian played a more circumscribed part in such activities. His goal was to be a nobleman or a priest, callings which, once attained or taken up, were regarded as inherent to the person, beyond the power of renunciation or cancellation. Victimized by nobles, ecclesiastics, and Jews, the shapeless mass of the Christian commonalty was left outside this framework in a state of perpetual fermentation produced by the longing of its constituents to move up to the nobility through military enterprise and thus to become members of the ruling caste of lords. As the Cordovan Juan Ginés de Sepúlveda said: "In our Cordova no notice is taken of commerce, and it is considered the greatest distinction to excel at arms. And so, after the care of one's family, the greatest concern with agriculture, an occupation that is honorable and close to nature, and which usually strengthens the body and the spirit and prepares them for travail and for war: to such an extent that the ancients preferred labor in the fields to commerce, and the Romans took many consuls and dictators from the plough. . . . Let us not worry, then, if for the moment Cordova has citizens whose strength exceeds their opulence" (*De appetenda gloria,* Madrid edition, 1870, IV, 206). We can now understand the broad scope of the saying "Either prince or peasant" (*O corte o cortijo*), or of this one: "Church or sea or royal house" (*Iglesia, o mar, o casa real*). People aspired to be direct administrators of the faith, or to undertake adventures that would lead to lordship, or to serve the king in some way, comfortable in the realization that they were nobles and not plebeians.

The awareness of being a nobleman by birth was especially a Castilian trait. As concerns this, Castile embraced the ancient kingdoms of Castile, León, and Andalusia, not excluding the Basques, the most honest and honorable people of the Peninsula and always preferred by the Crown for positions of strict responsibility. The Count-Duke of Olivares, the *de facto* king of Spain more than was his lord King Philip IV between 1621 and 1643, bears this idea out. In his instructions concerning government, written in 1625 to quicken the mind of the frivolous and drowsy monarch, he says: "It seems to me much to the advantage of Your Majesty that those vassals [i.e., the Portuguese] should live in the hope that your Majesty . . . should hold your court in Lisbon for a certain continuous period of time. . . . I also deem it Your Majesty's obligation to employ persons of that kingdom in the service of this one, and particularly in embassies and viceroyalties, presidencies of the royal councils, and in some of the posts in the royal household. And I also think it a good thing to do this with the Aragonese, the Flemish, and the Italians . . . who regard themselves as foreigners." The Portuguese, he adds, resemble the latter-named peoples more than they do the Castilians. The Castilians comprise the best of the Spanish infantry, in which "one sees, along with their loyalty to their kings (greater than that of any other vassals), *the brio and liberty with which the sorriest commoner of Castile treats any lord or noble,* even though he be greatly unequal in power, showing in the wisdom of his impulse how much human hearts exceed human forces."

Olivares was thinking about how he could use the royal prestige to bring the *disjecta membra* of the Spanish dominions in Europe into a unified relationship. The Aragonese, including the Catalonians and Valencians, seemed to be foreigners as late as 1625. The nucleus of Spain was still Castile, as it had been since the tenth century, precisely because its men had been what Olivares said they were. The humblest peasant sensed that he was a member of the seignorial caste, a potential hidalgo. This notion seems to me to fit the reality better than the notion of Castilian democracy, in which democracy can have no strict meaning. The way of life in Castile was never democratic; perhaps it was, to some extent, in Aragon. The Castilians were governed seignorially by the best or more fortunate members of the lordly caste, all of whose members aspired to the same privilege. This was the basis of its grandeur and of its final wretchedness. There was never any democracy in Castile in the Greek or the Franco-English sense of the word. The inverse case, although similar in its vital scheme, was presented by the Jews, who were prisoner-defenders of their own religious belief. The reason for their existence was also their religion, just as it was for the Hispano-Moslems. Nobility, industry, and labor: these three kinds of life existed in Spain, in the highest form, and "theoretically" there was no reason why a "normal" nation should not have been the result. But unfortunately this was not the case. It happened rather that the Jews became obsessed with the idea of becoming noblemen, and the Christians fell prisoners to the defensive, Inquisitorial tendency and the notion of purity of blood, going so far as to invent a new historical category, the "Old Christian."

The Christian had grown accustomed to having no need for a knowledge of nature and the handling of things, because this was not required in the huge task of conquering his land and organizing his state. The rest was left in the hands of Santiago, the French monks and immigrants, the Genoese shipbuilders, the Moorish builders of houses and fortresses, and the Jews, who knew trades, who could heal ailments, who knew how to collect the money to buy the things needed by the kings, the lords, the clerics, and the "good men" of the cities. The urgency of getting money explains why the Jew has always appeared in front of the footlights of history. The later importance of the precious metals of America was not the result of any economic doctrine: it was simply the sixteenth-century aspect of the need to acquire by indirect means the things that could not be created.

This way history is reclothed with meaning and explains

itself. For the Hispano-Christian, peace had never been productive. Juan de Lucena made a very shrewd observation in 1463. "There is no trouble around the house when the pigs are gone to the woods. . . . What a glorious king we would have, what a wonderful lot of vassals, what a crown for Spain, if the clergy, regular and secular, should go against Granada, and the king's knights should erupt into Africa! . . . *Increasing the number of kingdoms would produce greater wealth than the heaping up of treasures.*" The Christian in his own home felt himself with nothing to do, and he stirred up trouble in the kingdom. But once Granada was conquered, the great humanist Juan Ginés de Sepúlveda sensed a danger in the lack of an adequate enterprise in which the Spaniards might occupy themselves:

"According to the philosophers, nature, to enliven men's power, has endowed them with a certain inner fire which, if it is not poked and set to working, not only gives no light, but at times languishes and goes out. Therefore I sometimes wonder whether it would not have been better for us if the Moorish kingdom had not been preserved in Granada instead of disappearing completely. For if it is indeed certain that we have extended the kingdom, we have also thrown the enemy back beyond the sea, deprived the Spaniards of the opportunity to practice their valor, and destroyed the magnificent motive for their triumphs. Wherefore I fear a little lest, with so much idleness and security, the valor of many men grow weak."

Apparently the wars of Charles V were not enough for Sepúlveda. This idea, strange at first glance, has not been an isolated occurrence, for I find it again in Fray Alonso de Cabrera, preacher to Philip II:

"Our grandfathers, my lords, lamented the winning of Granada from the Moors, because on that day the horses fell lame and the cuirasses and lances began to rust, and the shields to rot. And the most distinguished cavalry of Andalusia was finished, and it was the end of youth and all its well-known gallantries."

The Spaniards had the liveliest kind of awareness that their existence was a process of self-creation and self-destruction. Ferdinand the Catholic, who knew his people well, offered them the bellicose, seignorial mission they longed for, the only thing they were really capable of. Then came the great enterprises in America and Europe, and the nation did not feel satisfied even with them, as we are told by Sepúlveda, Las Casas, Antonio de Guevara, Father Cabrera, Quevedo, and . . . Cervantes, well-qualified witness among many too numerous to mention. Gracián was to have the impression that he was living in an empty world, the same impression we get from the ascetics, the authors of the picaresque autobiographies, and Calderon's theatre.

The idea of castes whose only world is that of their own self-consciousness may explain this singular history. The guiding caste thought it could live alone, welded to its belief and its sense of superiority, and it noticed the irremediable vacuum in which it was submerged when it tried to come out of its incarceration in the self.

Prior to the sixteenth century no European country had produced such a profusion of heroes and chieftains who challenged the greatest obstacles nature could present, and always won—Vasco da Gama, Albuquerque, Cortes, Pizarro, Balboa, Magellan, Cabeza de Vaca, and a hundred others. Along with many friars fed by an equally titanic energy and illuminated by their religious belief, they ceaselessly consumed their selves as in a sacrificial holocaust to that strange deity, personal integralism, the whole living person. In opposition to the principle inherited from Greece that reality "is what it is," the Spaniard sustained the principle that reality was what he felt, believed, and imagined. "Having postponed fear"—a *leitmotiv* already in the fifteenth century—he installed himself in Italy, he rode victoriously over the heart of Europe and over the summits of the Andes. As he felt no fear, so he felt no surprise, for everything could be matched with fantasies already lived. Hernán Cortes' triumphal entry into Mexico seemed to his men like an episode from *Amadis,* or like an adventure with enchantment. Reality was a simple game with friendly or hostile wizards.

Will, courage, and imagination took the place of reflection, and created a form of life which it would be inept to characterize as primitive, backward, prescientific, etc. For this form of life developed according to an ascending scale of values. So-called "primitive" man is not aware of the risk he runs by being primitive. The Spaniard has always realized the high price he has had to pay for being Spanish.

·   ·   ·

The Hispano-Christian entered his history with the dangerous feeling that it was possible for him, in one burst of energy, to scale its greatest heights. As early as the year 1000, the Castilian was beginning to think that he could really "take" the Moor, and that fabulous Cordova was within reach of his sword. The conquests of Toledo and Valencia (although the latter conquest was temporary) provided an eleventh-century confirmation of his feeling of superiority, based on an awareness of his "intrinsic value." The Archpriest of Hita was later to say: "It is by serving well that Spanish knights win victories." To serve well as a knight was in fact a supreme aspiration. A person's value depended upon the vigor of his conduct in this regard. This attitude predisposed the Hispano-Christian to adopt whatever might reinforce it, even to the point of raiding the spiritual camp of the enemy. Thus he was ready to adopt Arabic ways of expressing personal value (*fijodalgo*), or what there was good in Arabic actions (*fazaños*). *Fazaña,* "feat, prowess," originally "model of goodness, generous act," comes from the Arabic *hasanah* (good act, generosity).

Fijodalgo and *fazaña* are clear evidence of the impression of superiority which the Moslem left with the Hispano-Christian a thousand years ago. Then, the Christian's feeling of superiority grew stronger and stronger. This must be the point of departure for understanding the inordinate urge to nobility and the sense of caste that took possession of the Hispano-Christian. I shall begin by citing texts that will put us in contact with the living reality of history. In a proclamation made in Valencia in 1410 against blasphemers who "soiled their lips and tongues by speaking ill of God and the Virgin Mary," plebeians were condemned to be publicly flogged and pilloried; "but if it be a *person of honor who does not work with his hands,* let him pay as a penalty fifty gold *maravedís.*" An abstract conception of history would treat such an idea as a "theme" or "commonplace," and would relate it to Plato's contempt for physical labor and his low regard for crafts, which reappears in the Middle Ages: *"Opus humanum, quod natura non est, sed imitatur naturam, mechanichum, i.e., adulterinum vocatur."* But what good would it do here to compose a study of the contempt for manual labor through the ages? We are actually faced with a kind of people who composed their existence out of the vital "impossibility" of working at tasks deemed not honorable. "You have always kept me busy with the base things of your mechanical job," says the soul to the body in the *Diálogos de la fantástica filosofía de los tres en uno.* The author could and may have taken his idea from a repertory of medieval commonplaces, but in its historical context the idea has a peculiarly Spanish meaning, for it implies that great value is attached to that which was not mechanical work, that is, the *intrinsic value* of the person.

That value was not only a matter of high spirit, courage, or *brío* predicted as attributes of the person. It was the very substance of the person, that which made him whole, all of a piece. The Spaniard has been the only example in Western history of a man whose purpose in life is founded on the idea that the only calling worthy of a man is to be a man, and nothing more. When Pedro Crespo entrusts his son to the general, Don Lope de Figueroa, he reasons thus: "What would he do here with me but idle his time away in a life of profligacy? Let him go and serve the king." Pedro Crespo, a successful peasant, feels that the value of his prosperity lies not in the fact that his life has been materially productive but in the fact that his wealth will assure his son a career in the ennobling service of the king.

No other European country so stigmatized manual labor, which was not accorded legal dignity until the reign of Charles III in the eighteenth century, in the course of the invasion of rationalist ideas from foreign lands, an invasion which affected only the epidermis of Spanish life. But it is also certain that belief in intrinsic value was continually shaken by the worry of those who found themselves locked up in their consciousness of caste as well as by the similar worry of those who realized the grave dangers of Spanish exclusivism. Pedro Fernández de Navarrete writes: "This court has been filled with many other persons of low degree: lackeys, coachmen, saddle boys, water-carriers, wafer peddlers, porters. . . . The harm that comes from the fact that these people are leaving the work in the fields undone need not be emphasized." The porter is singled out for special censure: "With the introduction of this not very ancient occupation, it has begun to be the custom that, if a servant buys a *real's* worth of fruit, he must give half to the porter who carries it, an extravagance tolerated only at the court of Spain." This criticism is closely connected with another: "No sooner has a merchant or a worker or a peasant enough to buy a government pension worth 500 ducats a year than he buys with this income a pension for his eldest son, whereupon not only this son but all his brothers become ashamed to occupy themselves at the humble tasks with which that money was originally earned," for "those who are not nobles aspire to make themselves nobles, and those who are aspire to rise to higher places still" (*ed. cit.,* pp. 473, 475).

In 1541 there were already in Castile and León 781,582 tax-paying commoners and 108,358 hidalgos; that is, 13 percent of the families in the kingdom paid no taxes and performed no work of any kind, and they lived like a closed caste. It was observed, however, that it was not possible "to preserve in good condition a republic that consists entirely of nobles, for, to assure mutual assistance between citizens, it is necessary to have a head to rule, priests to pray, counselors to counsel, judges to judge, noblemen to give orders, soldiers to defend, farmers to till, tradesmen to do business, and artisans to take care of mechanical matters." The last two classes of activity had been precisely the ones that had belonged to the Moors and Jews.

When the Spaniards got to the Indies, they implanted and perpetuated their way of life there. In 1590 the inhabitants of Buenos Aires wrote to Philip II in desperation, complaining of the poverty of the Argentine land (which for the English Puritans would have been a paradise), because it is not the land that makes the man but the reverse, even though the importance of natural conditions and the historical moment are not to be denied. In Argentina there was no gold or silver, nor were there native cities, as there were in Mexico and Peru, and the Spaniard, incapable of creating things, did not know what to do: "We are so poor and needy that we could not be more in want, in proof of which, *we do our plowing and digging with our hands*. . . . Such is the need from which the settlers suffer that *their own women and children bring their drinking water from the river*. . . . Spanish women, noble and of high quality, because of their great poverty *carry their drinking water* on their own shoulders." The superior of the Franciscan convent who was the author of this letter, sorrowfully confirms that "the people do their own work and [take care] of their cattle *with their own hands*, for I have seen it happen thus, and it is a pitiable state of affairs; the people wait on themselves as if it were the tiniest village in Spain."

I know no document more significant, especially for making understandable the history of Hispano-America and the contrasts it presents with the rest of America. The Spaniard moved into the region of the Plata in the sixteenth century just as in the tenth and eleventh he had spread down over the south of the Iberian Peninsula, with the object of gaining honor and maintaining seigniory for himself. Since there were neither Moors nor Jews to do the work in Buenos Aires, and since the Indians quickly fled out into the pampas, what was eventually to become the Argentina we know today remained in rather a wretched condition until about a century ago. Houses in Buenos Aires were straw-covered adobe huts, for this was the only kind of masonry the conquistador knew how to obtain without his wealth and his vassals to carry out his orders. As late as 1852, the future city was a pest-ridden village: "the skeletons of oxen and horses lay about in the mud in the middle of the street; even in front of the doors of some of the houses you could see the putrefied remains of animals."

But at the same time people in America and Europe were already familiar with *Facundo,* a brilliant historico-critical picture of Argentine life by Sarmiento, for to produce such a work of personal integration and expression there was no need of debasing manual labor. But work with the hands was precisely what Sarmiento was later to propose as the remedy for his country's ills, a program similar to that proposed in Spain by the licentiate Fernández de Navarrete in 1626: bring people in from the outside, make others work, give foreigners special privileges, let them "make the rivers navigable and dig ditches for irrigation. . . . The children of these foreigners would, in the second generation, be Spaniards who would fill out the population of Spain, which is the object toward which this discourse is directed" (p. 478). He went so far as to advocate the importation of Negroes "to improve some of the many mines that Spain possesses." These Negroes would, "by the second or third generation be white; if they were not, it would make no difference, since they were apt at manual labor and the cultivation of the soil" (p. 482). Fernández de Navarrete foresaw what was to happen in Brazil.

At first glance, Fernández de Navarrete's program looks like an attempt to correct the course of Hispanic history.

More closely examined, it turns out to be the contrary. His negative criticism and lamentations over the poverty and depopulation of the land could have been the utterances of any representative of the "Enlightenment," with the sole difference that the author did not in the least suspect that the lack of things, the sense of emptiness, belonged to the very direction of Spanish life. The proposed solutions were of a mechanical nature, requiring the addition of an element rather than the fundamental changing of any existing element in Spanish life, that is, they called for the addition of people to do what the Moors and Jews had long been doing without any thought that the dominant caste would cease to be what it was. That it was the working castes that were missed is clearly seen in this statement of utopian and nostalgic longing: "I am persuaded that if before the Moors and Jews had reached the state of desperation that brought them into such bad odor, a way had been found to admit them to certain honors, to avoid keeping them under the brand and stigma of infamy, it would have been possible for them to enter *through the door of honor* into the temple of virtue and into the bosom and obedience of the Catholic Church" (p. 466). This is in agreement with the ideas of Duart Gómez . . . Fernández de Navarrete's ignorance of his own history and the rationalistic naïveté of the statement are obvious. He was also dreaming of a unique utopian caste, without realizing that if the Moors and Jews should have attained an awareness of their "intrinsic value," they would have ceased to do the work whose lack was now ruining Spain.

In fine, this excellent treatise is discreet throughout and is full of the anguish of a person who sees clearly what the situation is and would like it to be different. But Fernández de Navarrete is like the madman in the asylum (*Don Quixote*, II, 1) who, just after he was adjudged sane and was about to leave, said to one of his fellow-inmates: "If that man is Jupiter and won't rain, I, who am Neptune . . . shall rain whenever I feel like it." According to Fernández de Navarrete's advice to the king, the pursuit of letters "usually engenders a certain melancholy that weakens the spirit by opposing the cheerful impulsiveness with which dangerous adventures are undertaken when reflection does not cause them to lag. And that is why the goddess of knowledge was called 'Minerva, *quasi minuens nervos*'[!], for the peoples that indulge excessively in the pleasure of learning easily forget the practice of arms. Spain has examples enough of this, *for as long as the ejection from Spain of the Saracens' heavy yoke lasted, she was raw and lacking in letters,* and to remedy this the universities and schools were founded by the kings" (p. 542)—as a foreign importation, it might be added.

Similar observations might be made about the writings of Diego de Saavedra Fajardo, Spain's representative at the preparatory conference for the Peace of Westphalia (1648) and a man widely read, widely traveled, and well-versed in foreign languages. He too laments the harm and poverty suffered by his country, and we might expect to find in him an advocate of Europeanization ready to shatter the forms of traditional Spanish life. But nothing of the kind. When the time comes to face the decisive issues, Don Diego feels like a Spaniard of the tenth century. His world is the world of belief: "Don Juan de Austria commanded his banners to be embroidered with the cross and this motto: 'With these arms I have conquered the Turks; with them I expect to conquer the heretics!' . . . I avail myself of them and of the standard of Constantine to signify to the princes the confidence with which they should raise the banner of religion against their enemies. . . . Heavenly spirits will attend this banner; *two riding on white horses* were seen fighting in the vanguard when King Ramiro II conquered the Moors near Simacas. . . . At the battle of Mérida in the time of King Alfonso IX there appeared that divine lightning bolt, Santiago, the son of thunder, the patron of Spain leading the squadrons with his blood-stained sword."

This belief, genuinely Spanish, was the sap and bark of the tree of Spanish life. Those who have been part of it include Quevedo, Gracián, and all those who have expressed something of what they have felt about themselves and Spain. Belief, not thought, intrinsic value, the sense of nobility, the spirit of caste, one and the same thing—the triple-stranded contexture of Christians, Moors, and Jews, 900 years old.

10

JAIME CORTESÃO

THE PORTUGUESE IMPRINT UPON BRAZIL

In contrast to the figure of the hidalgo whom Sánchez-Albornoz and Américo Castro have chosen to represent the ethos of late medieval Castile, Jaime Cortesão suggests in this selection that the sailor was the archetypical Portuguese of the Age of Discovery. Exposed to the sea to a degree unequaled by any other people of the peninsula, the Portuguese, he argues, created their empire in response to geographic imperatives and in this way affirmed and preserved their identity. Only through the acquisition of an empire could Portugal strengthen itself sufficiently to withstand the peninsular imperialism of Castile and thus retain the independence that it first found under the leadership of Afonso Henriques in the course of the twelfth century.

Jaime Cortesão (1884–1960) was the greatest historian of his generation in Portugal. After 1927 he lived mainly in exile in Brazil, where he embarked

From Jaime Cortesão, "Os factores democráticos na formação de Portugal," *Obras completas*, I (Lisbon: Portugália Editora, 1964), excerpted from pp. 247–265. Translated and printed by permission of Carolina Cortesão.

upon a study of the bandeirantes *whom he saw as continuing on land the Portuguese frontier spirit that first awoke during the age of discovery. Always rich in hypotheses and suggestions, and particularly sensitive to the interrelationship of geography and history, his most important works are his monumental study of* Os descobrimentos portugueses *and his multivolume work on* Alexandre Gusmão e o tratado de Madrid.

In recent years, two of Spain's greatest historical intellects, although differing as to the manner in which they think the essential structure of Spain should be defined, still agree on one point: according to them, the formation of Portugal as an independent state was the result of chance, a mere accident, the bitter fruit of unfortunate circumstances.

In order to be more aware of the importance of their opinions, let us note that the two historians Américo Castro, a philosopher and cultural historian, and Claudio Sánchez-Albornoz, an eminent medievalist—both come from liberal backgrounds, and both have liberal inclinations. They are not blinded by belated longings for empire; and their work, in spite of fundamental differences, shows clear understanding and vast erudition. The former, in *España en su história, Cristianos, Moros, y Judíos* (1948), includes a chapter with the suggestive title, "They Made Portugal Independent," while the latter's polemical work, *España, un enigma histórico* (1957), meant to refute the conclusions of the former, also contains a chapter called, "Portugal: an Historic Accident," which does not differ in interpretation from the first.

For Américo Castro, the birth of Portugal came about as a result of the personal ambitions of Count Henry of Burgundy, who had the vigorous political support of Hugh, abbot of Cluny, and of the House of Burgundy, as well as from the weakness of King Alfonso VI of Castile, who was struggling amidst the terrible difficulties of a civil war. Without the aid of the Burgundian counts, Portugal would not have come to exist as an independent nation.[1] This, in general, is his thesis. From this viewpoint, Sánchez-Albornoz does not dissent, either in the title of his chapter or in its depreciative tone. . . . According to him, Portugal came into being through the ambitious maneuvering of Count Henry of Burgundy and his wife Dona Teresa, who took successful advantage of the civil warfare that disturbed the reign of Queen Urraca of Castile, as well as through the political talent, energy, and military capability of their son [Afonso Henriques]. "Few moments in history," he writes, "could have been more propitious for the separation of a human community ruled by a capable and audacious leader." The creation of Portuguese independence was, then, in his opinion, the poisonous fruit of civil war.

Within this current of opinion, an extremist, Oswald Spengler, the illustrious author of *The Decline of the West*, goes so far as to say that without the arrival of Count Henry in Spain, Brazil would not exist today, thus implying that Brazil, a state of Portuguese origin, and the Luso-Brazilian community itself . . . are happenstance constructions that would never have existed without the exalted fantasies of a Clunias abbot and the ambitions of a Burgundian count. But here we are in the midst of a delirium of error in thinking that a nation can be born from a mere act of individual will, can be a product of

---

[1] Alfonso VI, King of León and Castile (1072–1109) married his two daughters to knights from the ducal house of Burgundy: the elder, Urraca, to Raymond; the younger, Teresa, to Henry. To the latter couple he also gave the administration of the part of his kingdom then called Portugal. Upon the death of Alfonso VI, Urraca became Queen, her husband Raymond having already died. The chronic civil wars of her reign, however, permitted her sister Teresa and Henry of Burgundy to defy Urraca's authority and to convert their territory of Portugal into an independent kingdom, de facto. (Ed.)

fortuitous circumstances, detached from all conditions of geography, economic peculiarities, and spiritual antecedents. Nevertheless, the indisputable authority of the first two authors, true masters of Spanish history and thought, and the literary prestige of Spengler, merit our special attention. Is there, in what they say, the whole, or at least a part of the truth?

. . .

It is undeniable that the prehistory, the protohistory, and to a lesser degree, the history itself of the Iberian peoples reveal a basic community of culture. The history of Portugal, like that of Aragon or of Castile, can only be understood within the framework of a common scheme, . . . Portuguese and Castilians, Galicians and Andalusians, are all branches of the same tree, grandchildren of the same forefathers, and those who try to deny this profound Hispanic brotherhood deny themselves a part of their own humanity. We do not hesitate to underline a phrase of Sánchez-Albornoz: "the successes and the defeats of each of the Hispanic peoples are shared by all of them." This admitted by way of preface, are Castro, Sánchez-Albornoz, and Spengler correct when they carry the community of prehistoric culture and Iberian brotherhood implicit in the history of the peninsula to its ultimate consequences? In fact, Sánchez-Albornoz accuses contemporary Portuguese who refuse to admit the fortuitous character of their nation's birth of suffering from the blight of nationalism. Possibly we should ask instead if the two eminent Spanish thinkers are not suffering from the cancer of imperialism, an endemic malady always prone to spring to life in Castilian souls.

In spite of the respect that is owed to these two masters of thought and the admiration that we have for the pessimistic ideas of the third, it is clear that according to contemporary understanding of history, all of them proceed like a botanist who tries to define and classify a plant by uprooting it and studying it without the slightest reference to the soil in which it is nourished. To believe these three, the Portuguese state and people are abstract entities, peninsular in their one and only essence, and might just as well have arisen on the Atlantic coast, on the central *meseta,* or on the Mediterranean shore of the Iberian peninsula. They immediately ignore this fundamental truth: the further back one goes into the past of man, the more his history is molded by geography. A famous contemporary historian, Ferdinand Braudel, even invented a neologism—geohistory—to designate the first ages of man when he lives in strict obedience to the determinants of his physical environment. Only later, little by little, does man liberate himself from this fatalistic pressure to bring a creative will into his life and to humanize the earth. But geography prefigures history, and the living lineage of a people sinks its roots into the soil from which they are born.

Thus it was from the close interpenetration of the sea and the land that the Portuguese came to be born with their characteristic way of life, their national character, their language, their religious sensibility, and—as the supreme product of the native spirit—their artistic expression.

To such an extent, in fact, was the formation of Portugal as an independent state *not* the mere product of circumstance, that amongst the negative digressions of Américo Castro, a glimmer of truth emerges when he says, "Portugal was born and grew through her desire *not* to be Castile," adding ". . . to this it owes not only its indubitable greatness, but also a great deal of its misery." If Portugal was born and grew through the wish *not* to be Castile, where, then, we may ask, did it acquire this pertinacious will?

The reply, or rather the mere beginnings of an answer, is provided by Sánchez-Albornoz when he affirms that Afonso Henriques began by "exploiting the animosity of the Portuguese and the Galicians to increase the localistic feeling of his people." And if there was a localistic sentiment that made the Portuguese hostile to the Galicians, how much stronger was it when directed against the Leónese and the Castilians.[2] But this reference to a localistic, anti-Galician feeling is, in the end, merely a depreciative way of hiding a fundamental reality. What really gave force to the group led by Count Henry of Burgundy and later by his son was a pre- and protonationalistic sentiment in the Atlantic West of Iberia. Between the Luso-Galicians north of the Tagus and the Mozárabes[3] to the south, there existed a community of culture and feeling that was already revealed in the close relationship between their two dialects, distinct from the language spoken on the central *meseta*. The Portuguese kings, from Afonso I (1139–1179) to Afonso III (1245–1279) could conquer and secure their control over the provinces of the south thanks to a continual cooperation of the Mozárabic population. Count Sesnando in the central part of the country, Gonçalo Sem-Pavor in the Alentejo, and Garcia Rodrigues in the Algarve are the historic representatives and symbols of this community, so old and solid that centuries of profound Islamic acculturation never succeeded in destroying it.

This Western brotherhood obeyed the general lines of geography and economy. Of all the peripheral regions of the Iberian peninsula—the Cantabrian coast, Catalonia, Murcia, Valencia, Andalusia, and the Atlantic shore—none was more different from the central *meseta* than Portugal due to its more intimate and prolonged contact with the sea. A great number of Portugal's geographic characteristics are rooted in what we might call an "Atlantic convergence." Above all, its geographic position at the southwestern tip of Europe beside the sea route

---

[2] Throughout the essay the author assumes that the reader knows that medieval Portugal and Galicia were culturally very similar while there were marked cultural differences between Portugal and León-Castile. (Ed.)

[3] Christians living under Muslim rule. (Ed.)

formed by the Canary Current and the northeasterly winds
made its ports (aside from being mandatory way stations
along the sea routes that unite southern and northern
Europe) the best points of embarkation for Africa, Central
and South America, and Asia. Even after the settlement of
the archipelagos of the Azores and the Cape Verde Islands,
Portugal still possessed the European areas closest to the
New World, excellent ports of call and naval bases for
reaching the American continent. Indented at frequent
intervals by estuaries both large and small, a geographic
highway close to and parallel to this western seaway established communication between the north and south of
Portugal, thus facilitating the formative unity of its human
nuclei.

The German geographer Theobald Fischer was of the
opinion (shared by J. Brunhes) that "the geograpic situation of an independent Portugal in relation to Spain was
similar to that of an independent Holland with regard to
Germany," emphasizing that "no other region of the peninsula was so intimately linked to the sea, which penetrated
profoundly into the interior, via its great estuaries." The
two geographers would have been even more sure of their
idea had they known that during the medieval period
almost all the estuaries of Portuguese rivers were larger
and deeper, permitting a greater contact between man and
the sea, and that many ports, which then existed, completely disappeared at a later date due to the transforma-
tions over the centuries that have made the Portuguese
coastline more regular. Before the estuaries of the [main
Portuguese rivers] had been progressively silted up, these
rivers could be navigated deep into Portuguese territory.
And by a happy chance of nature, an admirable bay
defended by a narrow estuary in the middle of the western
coast permitted Lisbon to capture this sea traffic and to
take direction of the Portuguese state. At the right moment
it became the great maritime and cosmopolitan metropolis
of the West, where products were concentrated and influ-

ences coming from Europe, Africa, America and Asia were blended.

Issuing out from this great concentration of sea routes, Portuguese expansion in the world was accomplished via the great natural lines of intercontinental navigation traced by the winds and the currents. Before discovering and colonizing other worlds, Portugal discovered and traced the routes that led to them. When the Portuguese, in order to colonize the Azores and to communicate with the fortified factories of Arguim and El Mina,[4] discovered the cyclonic winds and currents of the mid-Atlantic basin, which describe a kind of ellipse between the coasts of Portugal, the Caribbean sea, and back again, they had already traced the pattern upon which the first voyage of Columbus was to be based. In turn, the Portuguese creation of Brazil was implicit in the northeasterly winds that arise on the coasts of Portugal and in the southern equatorial current that irresistibly drags sailing ships to the coasts of Brazil. The foundation of Mozambique, as well as of Luanda in Angola afterward, came about from the advantage taken of these two ports of call along the maritime routes from Lisbon to India and from Brazil to Africa.

Likewise, the Portuguese, in creating Brazil as it exists today, adapted themselves to the unity of the great interior tropical forest that spreads out between the basins of the Amazon and La Plata and that was equally the home of a prehistoric and indigenous cultural unity. The geography and cultural anthropology of that continent prefigured, before the coming of Cabral, the Brazilian state. To have given, in all these cases, political and human expression to the determinants of nature, through the will *not* to be Castile, or rather through the simple desire to be itself— this is the greatest factor in Portuguese independence, the great affirmation, if you will, of the national genius. And since poetry is one of the best ways to capture hidden reality, let us resort to some verses of Camões:

---

[4] Along the Atlantic coasts of Africa. (Ed.)

> Here you have, almost at the summit
> Of Europe's head, the Lusitanian realm
> Where the Land ends and the Sea begins
> And where Phoebus reposes in the Ocean.[5]

But let us make a slight correction in this stanza of the Epic. It is in *Spain* that the land comes to an end; only in Portugal does the ocean commence. Venus had more than sufficient reason to protect the Lusitanians as she does in the poem. Brothers of the goddess Anadyomene, they too were born of the sea.

The history of Portugal has developed from the human and geographical bases of its pre- and protohistory. The Celtic Lusitanians, Romanized and Christianized according to their own tendencies, are the oldest ancestors of the Portuguese; and almost immediately they distinguished themselves from the peoples of the Spanish *meseta*. The characteristic Portuguese way of life—that is to say, long distance maritime commerce—was learned from the Normans and the Arabs. Stretching along the whole shoreline, this trade . . . extended to the Mediterranean and Atlantic ports of Europe and became the vital impulse for the Discoveries. The Portuguese language, whose original characteristics appear as early as the tenth century, gained through its specific locution the flavor of nautical life. And descending from the religion of the Celts and from Priscillianism, so impregnated with laicism and the love of nature, a profoundly Franciscan Christianity, gave religious sanction to the overseas expansion of the Portuguese.

These influences were projected overseas in the human creations of that expansion. The "State of Brazil," as Gabriel Soares de Sousa already called it in the last quarter of the sixteenth century, followed in its origins the same kind of life that was typical of the Portuguese nation. For Brazil too was born beside the sea, with the planting of

---

[5] *Os Lusíadas,* canto 3, stanza 20. (Ed.)

sugar cane and an international seaborne commerce in
sugar. An identical spiritual education marked its history.
Even the phenomenon of the *Bandeirantes*—that is to say,
the expansion of Brazil outward to its natural frontiers
(the fact that, according to Ruy Barbosa, best defines
Brazilian history)—bears the mark of a Portuguese origin.
Ruy Barbosa and Alcântara Machado speak of the profound identity between the sailor and the *sertanista*.[6] The
latter pointed out that the captain of the *banda* was called
the *armador,* and the preparation for the expedition the
armação, as if one were speaking of ships; and that the
bandeira was also called a "fleet" or "discovery."

Let us recall, for our part, that *varar* and *varação* in the
varadouro (a maneuver for the portage of canoes from one
river to another), a common practice among the *bandeirantes,* are nautical terms; that the map of the route of the
bandeira was called a *roteiro;* that the "monsoons," fleets
of canoes, which left at a certain season from São Paulo
for the Mato Grosso, took the name of the alternating
winds of the Indian Ocean where the Portuguese had
created the word on the basis of an indigenous linguistic
root; and that the Minas Gerais, like the Campos Gerais of
the state of Paraná, evokes the same word as that used by
Portuguese pilots to designate the alternating winds that
blow repeatedly over the vast regions of the oceans. In a
document from the beginning of the eighteenth century,
the writer speaks of the "seaside" of the gold mines and of
the Campos Gerais, "which are commonly called the
backwash." Finally there is the name of *restingas,* given to
isolated hilly formations in the countryside and to the slag
heaps where the poorest people went to mine. That is to
say, all the words that signify method, organization, continuity, and those that define characteristics of production
and accidents of relief are Portuguese words imported from
seafaring: they place on the development of the *bandeiras*

---

[6] *Sertanista,* an explorer of the Brazilian interior. See Richard
M. Morse, *The Bandeirantes* (New York, 1962). (Ed.)

the indelible mark of a people of nautical culture; and they reveal in the *bandeirantes* a sense of space, enriched by interoceanic voyages. Portuguese and Brazilians, become *bandeirantes,* remained faithful to the sea and to the language of seafaring. They come to "navigate" the backlands in human "fleets" to the certain rhythm of the "monsoons," and keeping wide of the "generals," they cross the "reefs" to the sterile limits from whence they return in the "backwash."

This essential continuity is no less remarkable from the religious point of view. A great Brazilian historian, Capistrano de Abreu, postulated with masterful authority that the history of Brazil could not be written until we know the history of the Jesuits. This opinion errs only in what it omits, for it would have been more correct to say that the history of Brazil cannot be written without knowing the history of *all* the religious orders that influenced the spirit of the Portuguese and Brazilians, helped to convert the Indians to a sedentary existence, attenuated the shock of contact between the native and the newcomer, and aided the civilians who tamed the wilderness in order to place far in the backlands the boundary markers that created the frontiers of Brazil. It seems to us that the role that is usually attributed to Ignatius of Loyola in the spiritual development of Brazil is due rather to Saint Francis. It will be said that the Franciscans did not play as extensive or intensive a role in Brazil as did the Jesuits. That is true. But to the extent (and this was decisive) that Portugal contributed to the development of Brazil, this participation was accomplished under the inspiration of Saint Francis.

The Portuguese, whose national character was developed during the first centuries of its history, were educated in two schools—that of errant knighthood, disciplined and directed against Islam, and that of the Franciscans—two strong foundations for the activity of a people meant to discover and colonize other worlds. Through the spirit of knighthood the Portuguese are linked with the Spanish; through Franciscanism they are set apart. Both peoples are capable of shouldering a lance like Don Quixote to fight and lose themselves for an ideal: but while the Spanish, through an innate tendency to go beyond reality, are always prone to attack the giants they imagine to be lurking behind the sails of the windmill, the Portuguese, more humble and humane, would rather, on passing by, rest their lance by the doorway and take advantage of the moment to mill their grain.

Basically this is the same difference as that between Saint Ignatius and Saint Francis. One wishes to triumph, to exalt, and to glorify God *ad majorem dei gloriam*—the program of a militia that does not avoid, but rather seeks out combat; the other—to realize Christ on earth through a return to the simple and humble virtues of the Bible. Whatever there may be in Brazil, or in Portugal, of loving brotherhood, of toleration, of comprehension of foreigners, confident optimism, joy, and generous effusion, of salt-of-the-earth simplicity, derives from the Franciscan Christianity in which the Portuguese of all classes from the king to the humblest villein, were educated for centuries.

A symbol of this education was and still is the cult of Saint Anthony (or rather Saint "Tony"), so solidly rooted in the hearts of the Portuguese and Brazilian people. Not the historic saint, but rather the one that was molded and sweetened according to the popular Franciscan model of sanctity. During the four centuries of its history the two most popular cults in Brazil were St. Anthony and that of the Holy Spirit, both of medieval Portuguese origin. And Franciscanism, although a creation of the Middle Ages, really symbolized the dawn of the Renaissance, and thus of Brazil.

Such are the reasons that lead us to propose this rectification of history: Franciscanism was and is the soul of Brazil—the primitive seed that resisted so many storms and grown until today; the impulse that moved from the first mass recited by a Franciscan on the Island of the Red Crown in Porto Seguro to the civic orations of Ruy

Barbosa defining the civil and liberal spirit; the sense of American solidarity; and the universalism of Brazilian civilization—just as it is of the Portuguese.

. . .

In discussing the causes that determined our expansion overseas, one often forgets one of the most essential reasons, which might be formulated in the following manner. The Portuguese went out to discover and colonize foreign lands in order to conserve their own. The struggle with the seas was a continuation of Aljubarrota,[7] just as the latter was already a revindication of Portugal's personality as an Atlantic nation. It has been said, and with reason, that when they discovered the maritime route to India after three-quarters of a century of effort, the Portuguese succeeded in resolving one of the gravest problems bequeathed to Europe by the Middle Ages: that of commerce with the Orient, blocked since the thirteenth century by the progressive expansion of Muslim power. But, perchance, the solution of the problem was not of immediate interest to us? Certainly it was of vital interest for the Italian republics of Venice and Genoa, or for the Aragonese Confederation, for whom the oriental trade was the basis of riches and power; but Portugal, as a mere port of call along the trade routes of the Mediterranean and the Atlantic, was only indirectly interested and then in a minor way. Nevertheless, from a geographic point of view, from the point of view of its Atlantic vocation, no other country combined such favorable conditions to undertake the solution of this great problem of world commerce. Portugal was, potentially, the base for Western expansion and for the unification of humanity. The political and economic conjuncture,

---

[7] The battle that the Portuguese won at Aljubarrota against invading Castilian forces in 1385 secured the nation's independence until 1580. (Ed.)

both national and international, along with the spirit of Franciscan Christianity, in love with nature, impelled it to realize that mission.

What would have happened if the Portuguese nation had not undertaken the role that geography indicated? To tell the truth, the external situation of Portugal at the beginning of the fifteenth century was particularly unfortunate, given the proximity of the rival nation of Castile. The latter, which had already been defeated in its first attempt to absorb us, was ready to take advantage of any and all occasions to agrandize itself and to weaken us. Although they did not possess the same geographic advantage as did the Lusitanian shoreline, nevertheless Seville and the neighboring ports along the mouth of the Guadalquivir, as well as those of the Cantabrian sea, maintained at this time an extensive and intensive maritime commerce and could become the basis for a movement of geographic expansion, an expansion that had in fact already begun with Castilian attempts to dominate the navigation of the Straits of Gibraltar and with her conquest of the Canary Islands. If the Portuguese had not initiated, in 1415, their plan of territorial and maritime expansion with the conquest of Ceuta, it would probably have been executed by Castile. And Portugal, without its own fructifying sense of nationhood, would have sooner or later regressed to the . . . status of a simple provincial division of Iberia, destined to furnish sailors to an imperial Spain in the full process of expansion overseas.

But Castile was torn by struggles between the king and feudal nobility and blocked to the south by the Moorish kingdom of Granada, whose conquest was a preliminary condition of its expansion into Morocco and the Atlantic. On the contrary, the Portuguese, in the full flower of democratic government in their town councils, had acquired an admirable political unity thanks to the will to be free and uniquely themselves. And the sea—*that* was their kingdom of Granada!

Had they not, beginning with the Master of Aviz,[8] comprehended the necessity of anticipating the Castilians in the task of measuring the seas and occupying the way stations along the great maritime routes? The sense of danger from Castile was too sharp and their ability to confront it victoriously too well proven for the most enlightened and responsible Portuguese to renounce the guarantees of independence and greatness that the sea offered to them. It is enough to cast a glance over the internal situation of the country to understand that only a cause such as national independence could have launched us at that time on a movement of expansion. The kingdom of Portugal then counted a mere million or so inhabitants; moors, bogs, and wild forest covered the major part of the country; we were exceedingly poor in industry and needed to import most manufactured products; and the imperfectly evolved class structure formed a more balanced society. We ran the risk, with overseas ventures, of augmenting this disequilibrium, as indeed later happened. There was no lack of Old Sages with their eloquent advice. But the need to anticipate Castile in overseas expansion was imposed upon us by our essentially Atlantic character.

Today, more than five centuries later, it is still vitally necessary for us to remain faithful to the conditions of our independence. And when Sánchez-Albornoz in *España, un enigma histórico* denounces the antiscientific rationalism of some contemporary Portuguese historians, attributing this either to a lack of faith in "the value of a peoples' free will to dispose of their destinies" or to a fear of a crisis in national political structures "in the process of becoming wider human communities," perhaps there is some salutary advice, in these reflections of his, although they err by being divorced from reality and excessively general. That

---

[8] João I (1385–1433) was master of the military order of Aviz before becoming king. (Ed.)

the structure of Portugal overseas is undergoing, in the present world situation, grave risks, few are unaware. But we also suspect that not everyone knows the proper course to follow in facing the problem. Few times in our national history has it been more necessary to call the Portuguese people to a full realization of their obligations, adjusting ourselves, as we have said above, to the rhythm of the civilization to which we belong. And this in consultation, or rather in friendship and continuity, with Brazil—and the sooner the better.

BIBLIOGRAPHICAL NOTE

In addition to the books and articles in the footnotes to the Introduction, the interested student will find a complete and annotated bibliography to the books and articles on Iberian history published since 1953 in the *Indice histórico español* (Barcelona, 1953—), which is issued yearly. A convenient, though now somewhat dated, bibliographical introduction to the Iberian background problem is Charles Julian Bishko, "The Iberian Background of Latin American History: Recent Progress and Continuing Problems," *Hispanic American Historical Review*, XXXVI (1956), 50–80.

The Mediterranean background is best approached via the still useful chapter of Robert S. Lopez in *The Cambridge Economic History of Europe*, 2 vols. (Cambridge, 1952), II, 257–355, which includes a full bibliography up to that date. For work done since then, an excellent guide with ample bibliography can be found in Jacques Heers, *L'Occident aux XIVe et XVe siècles: aspects économiques et sociaux* (Paris, 1963), which covers not only the Mediterranean, but the rest of Europe too. In the same series (*Nouvelle Clio*) Pierre Chaunu has just published *L'Expansion européenne du XIIIe au XVe Siècle* (Paris, 1969) and *Conquête et exploitation des nouveaux mondes* (Paris, 1969), both with exhaustive bibliographies. On Barcelonese trade the reader has the benefit of two superb works from the Braudel school: Claude Carrère's *Barcelone, centre économique a l'époque des difficultés*, 1380–1462, 2 vols. (Paris, 1967), and Charles E. Dufourcq, *L'Espagne catalane et le Maghrib aux XIIIe et XIVe siècles* (Paris, 1966).

The economic history of late medieval Spain has been summarized with a wealth of hypothesis and information by Jaime Vicens Vives, *História económica de España* (Barcelona, 1959), pp. 143–265. Probably the best survey of other aspects of Spanish society in the later middle ages is to be found in Santiago Sobrequés Vidal, "Patriciado urbano," *História social y económica de España y América,* Jaime Vicens Vives (ed.), 2 vols. (Barcelona, 1957), II. For the various Iberian institutions that served as models for the creation of royal government in the Indies, the student should consult Luis García de Valdeavellano, *Curso de historia de las instituciones españolas desde los orígenes al final de la Edad Média* (Madrid, 1968), which summarizes the most recent research and provides an exhaustive bibliography.

On the Portuguese side, the reader has recourse to the detailed and excellent bibliography of Portuguese history (to 1500) prepared by A. H. de Oliveria Marques, *Guía do estudante de história medieval portuguêsa* (Lisbon, 1964). This may be supplemented by Bailey C. Diffie's *Prelude to Empire: Portugal Overseas Before Henry the Navigator* (Lincoln, Neb., 1960), which assembles in chronological fashion considerable information on Portuguese overseas trade up to circa 1415. Another work of importance is Manuel Nunes Dias, *O capitalismo monárquico português,* 2 vols. (Coimbra, 1963–1965).

The technical side of the expansion is expertly presented by J. H. Parry in *Age of Reconaissance* (Cleveland, 1963), although the author tends to limit his bibliography to works in English. For pertinent maps, the most lavish presentation is certainly Armando Cortesão e Avelino Teixeira da Mota, *Portugaliae monumenta cartographica,* 6 vols. (Lisbon, 1960); while on the Spanish side there is Marco Jiménez de la Espada (ed.), *Relaciones geográficas de Indias,* 4 vols. (Madrid, 1881–1887). Also useful is Duque de Alba y Julio Guillén, *Mapas españoles de América, Siglos XV–XVII* (Madrid, 1951).

A Note on the Type

The text of this book was set on the Linotype in a face called TIMES ROMAN, designed by Stanley Morison for *The Times* (London), and first introduced by that newspaper in 1932.

Among typographers and designers of the twentieth century, Stanley Morison has been a strong forming influence, as typographical advisor to the English Monotype Corporation, as a director of two distinguished English publishing houses, and as a writer of sensibility, erudition, and keen practical sense.

Composed, printed, and bound by
H. Wolff Book Manufacturing Co., Inc.
New York, N.Y.

BORZOI BOOKS ON LATIN AMERICA

Under the General Editorship of Lewis Hanke

THE CONFLICT BETWEEN CHURCH AND
STATE IN LATIN AMERICA *
Edited by Frederick B. Pike

THE MASTERS AND THE SLAVES (ABRIDGED)
A STUDY IN THE DEVELOPMENT
OF BRAZILIAN CIVILIZATION
By Gilberto Freyre

DO THE AMERICAS HAVE A COMMON HISTORY?*
A CRITIQUE OF THE BOLTON THEORY
Edited by Lewis Hanke

AMAZON TOWN
A STUDY OF MAN IN THE TROPICS
(*With a New Epilogue by the Author*)
By Charles Wagley

A VOYAGE TO SOUTH AMERICA (ABRIDGED) *
By Jorge Juan and Antonio de Ulloa
(*With an Introduction by Irving A. Leonard*)

AGRARIAN REFORM IN LATIN AMERICA *
Edited by T. Lynn Smith

THE BANDEIRANTES
THE HISTORICAL ROLE OF THE BRAZILIAN PATHFINDERS
Edited by Richard M. Morse

DICTATORSHIP IN SPANISH AMERICA *
Edited by Hugh M. Hamill, Jr.

THE ORIGINS OF THE LATIN AMERICAN
REVOLUTIONS, 1808–1826 *
Edited by R. A. Humphreys and John Lynch

THE EXPULSION OF THE JESUITS FROM
LATIN AMERICA *
Edited by Magnus Mörner

THE MONROE DOCTRINE *
ITS MODERN SIGNIFICANCE
Edited by Donald Marquand Dozer

* *Also available in a hardbound edition*

A DOCUMENTARY HISTORY OF BRAZIL *
Edited by E. Bradford Burns

BACKGROUND TO REVOLUTION *
THE DEVELOPMENT OF MODERN CUBA
Edited by Robert Freeman Smith

IS THE MEXICAN REVOLUTION DEAD? *
Edited by Stanley R. Ross

FOREIGN INVESTMENT IN LATIN AMERICA *
Edited by Marvin Bernstein

WHY PERON CAME TO POWER *
Edited by Joseph R. Barager

MARXISM IN LATIN AMERICA *
Edited by Luis E. Aguilar

A CENTURY OF BRAZILIAN HISTORY SINCE 1865 *
Edited by Richard Graham

REVOLUTION IN MEXICO: YEARS OF UPHEAVAL,
1910–1940 *
Edited by James W. Wilkie
and Albert L. Michaels

THE LIBERATOR, SIMON BOLIVAR: *
MAN AND IMAGE
Edited by David Bushnell

THE INDIAN BACKGROUND OF LATIN AMERICAN
HISTORY: *
THE MAYA, AZTEC, INCA, AND THEIR PREDECESSORS
Edited by Robert Wauchope

Forthcoming:

NATIONALISM IN LATIN AMERICA
Edited by Samuel L. Baily

* *Also available in a hardbound edition*